Copyright © 2017 Stacie Winkfield All rights reserved.
This book or parts thereof may not be reproduced in any form, stored in any retrieval system, or transmitted in any form by any means—electronic, mechanical, photocopy, recording, or otherwise—without prior written permission of the authors or publisher, except as provided by United States of America copyright law.

i

Acknowledgements

When I started writing my book, all that mattered was that I shared the message. I remember holding on tight to my renewed relationship with God and saying, "Even though it hurts, if I have to do it alone with You, God, then I will."

It has definitely been a tremendous journey to become the woman I am now from where I used to be. So, first and foremost I'd like to thank God. Thank You for instilling in me a vision. It wasn't always easy but it was always possible with Your voice to guide me, Your presence to hold me, and Your courage to push me to expand my level of consciousness.

Thank you to my girls, Geilah, Bella, and Guiliana. Thank you for your sacrifice of your mommy and our time, so that I could create a part of me to birth into the world, the same as I birthed you. Thank you for wiping Mommy's tears, for telling me to get back up when I fell repeatedly, and for reminding me that there is something bigger than my personal life and myself. Thank you for shaking me, for not letting the pain consume me, for saying, "Mommy, get up." If you want to change the world, you will.

Thank you to my editor, Andrea McCurry for capturing the voice of my work in ways I could have never imagined. Thank you to my coach, Vickie Gould, for seeing bigger things within me, that I was never taught or conditioned to see in myself. The level of support you two extend makes me proud to hold the same space. I am more aware because of you, because of the light you bring, and I have even further crafted that "thing" that only I can do.

And last but not least, thank you for every contributor to my story. Thank you for the laughs, and thank you for the tears. Thank you for standing by me no matter what, and thank you for leaving me. Thank you for not seeing in me what I saw in myself. If everyone had seen what I knew was there, they would have been along for the win and not the woman. My perception of our relationship could not have been experienced if we never shared time in space together. So I thank you for your time, no matter how brief or how long. I thank you for not believing in me, because it was your disbelief that pushed me to prove myself even more.

The pain made up my story, and I could not be who I am today, without the hurt of my yesterday.

So, thank you to Dawn. I may never see your face again, but I am resolute in knowing your love transcends dimensions. Thank you to Mama; you saved me. Even when I was unsure of your why, questioned your practices, denied your gift, and boasted in everything I thought was wrong, I never took the opportunity to thank you for all that was right. Thank you for everyone who left; you made room for new people, new opportunities, and new growth. And thank you Stacie; thank you for your hard work, thank you for your commitment, thank you for radical action, and most of all, thank you for your love.

Table of Contents

Preface

Chapter 1 – The Adoption

Chapter 2 – Change Your Story, Change Your Life

Chapter 3 – Heal Your Wounds Through Self-Love

Chapter 4 – What Makes You Special

Chapter 5 – Heal Yourself Intentionally

Chapter 6 – Radical Forgiveness

Chapter 7 – Remember Who You Really Are

Chapter 8 – The Power of Releasing Control

Chapter 9 – Intentional Faith

Chapter 10 – Do It Afraid

Afterward – Your God Spark

If No One Tells You Today: You Are Light, You Are Source, You Are God Manifested in the Flesh

This book began as my journal, a story for myself as the observer, about myself. I wrote the book that I searched through all the self-help shelves at the bookstores for. This is the book I couldn't find with Google, the one that I knew one day would awaken something inside of me, and even the one I asked other people around me about, but still couldn't get my hands on. I wrote the book I needed and couldn't find, the one that had no smiling face on the cover staring back at me. When I wrote this book, I wasn't yet in a place of transformation, I was in the emptiness, a place of despair, and I just wanted for someone to come and hold my hand, to hear me, to see me, and to acknowledge my pain. I needed someone to show me that I was not alone, and to help me find my way back home.

When the writing began to make me uncomfortable, I made every decision to never turn my back on it, and continued to work until it was complete. It was a commitment, it was discipline, and it was intentional. You see, for me, there was never a choice of either/or. There was no turning back to what I had known before, for nothing was waiting for me there but pain, disappointment, and depression. What was waiting for me there was what felt like a slow, unending death. [an emptiness, the great nothing]. My whole life was riding on this creation; in these moments, my life depended on finding my purpose as if it was my oxygen. And then, I realized why my life depended on the writing, because the writing was an ingredient for the antidote to heal my broken heart. The writing shed light into the darkness that consumed me for so long.

To be in the space where your life is dependent on your purpose is one full of pain and magic. Your darkest place is the birthplace to your greatest creation. There is something celestial about it, like when a dream that was left germinating inside of you one day awakens, like being pregnant. I began nurturing and growing my gift, sitting in my experience and pleasantly awaiting its birth. There was no, "what to expect when expecting," but I soon grew to figure it all out through the process.

Your dream will not come with an instruction manual. But you will realize just like I did, that you do not have to have everything right. You don't need all the people in the right place, at the right time before you begin. You are not required to have all of your finances tucked away neatly into conservative accounts that earn minimal gains off your investments, nor does anyone expect you to be perfect. Yet, so many of us expect perfection from ourselves. One of the most important things that is required of you, will be to find that thing that makes you feel most alive and to allow your finger to simply press the start button. The act of stepping out on faith in the unseen. A fire in your belly like never before. Your imperfection, that thing that made you feel alone, that need for love, that change in your career, that story you have in common with so many other souls you couldn't even imagine; that story doesn't even belong to you.

My life all came down to one qualitative point, one summary, one burning desire, one measure. And then, I became the writer of my destiny and a master builder in my life. And so, for you, I only have one question:

Do you have the courage to tear yourself down, in order to build yourself back up?

I asked myself, what was the worst that could happen if I took the steps towards starting to live a life that only I deemed worth living? I wanted to stand for something, and I wanted others to know what I stood for before I turned up my toes and let the time and space of this continuum consume me. I wanted others to see the flower beneath the surface bloom and be present when the offspring arrived. There was a beauty to my darkness that I so selfishly kept to myself for so long. My stories never belonged to me, but to all the people in the world; those who had been and sat in the darkness, waiting to be acknowledged, waiting to be heard, waiting to have a voice. Once I discovered this realization, I became ready and unapologetically willing to put in the work to make myself whole.

And so, I sought her, the whole me, not the version you see today, or the version from 20 years ago, or even the one from yesterday. I sought her, the 2027 version of myself, the great one that I knew I was destined to be. I started to emulate her, talk like her, walk like her, dress like her, and hold myself accountable to the standards of what I knew she would one day become. I became the woman that I had always wanted to be. I gave myself permission, to let my greater self, love and hug on my later self, so I could be comfortable handing the torch over to her, so she could run the rest of our race. I could no longer stay still in a career that no longer served me. I could no longer tell the past of broken stories as the only version of my truth. I couldn't even blame others for the failed relationships that I had chosen for myself. I had to move forward, out of the sorrow, through the layers of sheets and tear-stained pillowcases, and I had to hold myself accountable. This was the only road to redemption, to get me the help that I so deeply required.

And so, my call to action is for you to become the best version of yourself, to find that vision of yourself today. Don't look backwards on the vision of yourself from 10 or 15 years ago, or even the one you were yesterday. With each day, you have the power to show up...to create the best version of you. You have the power to become a Master Builder. Isn't God magnificent! He only made one you! I am so excited to see your gifts!

Aren't you sick and tired of being sick and tired? Are you willing to become so committed to your purpose, you would break your own heart? If so, let's begin to go out into the world and be that 2027 version of you. This is the version of you whose ready to show up and show out when challenges arise. You are brave, you are bold, and you are unique in your ability to bring gifts into the world. Let's start to manifest the life you were destined to live. Are you willing to become the man or woman you have always known yourself to be, so that other people may see themselves more clearly in relationship to you? If you are, then you and I can make all the difference between who we intend to be and who we really are. Because when you show up, when you play full-out, when you smile, it makes us all better. We may fall down, but if it wasn't for our breakdowns, we might never have had the opportunity to have our breakthroughs. And so, cheers to our breakthroughs! Together, we are all breaking bravely.

The tools I will teach you throughout this book, to get you through your darkest place, or maybe even many dark places, will not come from a pill bottle. My offering to you has no long list of potential side effects. The interactions of all things combined will not leave you having to monitor for symptoms. Instead, what you will be able to monitor, put your finger on, and have an explanation for is the capacity to love yourself and others in the world around you. This is a measurable love that bypasses the greatest of poets, hugs you like the best of parents, and reasons like the greatest of spouses. I am going to teach you how to fall madly in love with yourself.

When I became the writer of my story and not the victim of my negligence, my life, for the first time, thrived and became the most important thing in the world to me. All the love I gave to everyone else, I then realized was actually mine, so I began to take notice and return it all back to myself. I didn't need anyone to validate the work that I had done, because my validation was enough. I became aware that I was enough, and through that awareness I became transparent. This is the same prayer of transformation that I have in mind for you!

I could have chosen to stay depressed. I could have chosen to lay there in the sheets and soak in my sadness, as my children pressed into the small of my thigh and rocked it back and forth pleading, "Mommy, get up." I could have used antidepressants to fight off the darkness that consumed me. I could have gotten drunk or buried myself spoons-deep into a gallon of lactose-free ice cream, or I could have even done what most people do; sought a temporary bandage for a lifetime of pain through the distraction of a partner. However, from my career in nursing, I knew that a wound, not healed from the inside out, would only open back up and cause further complications.

Nothing from the outside, could fill the hole deep on the inside of me that was sure to come to the surface. Nothing from the outside can heal abandonment, mistrust, or the never-ending ache to be wanted, to be chosen, and to be loved. We wear it in our clothes like the smoke from cigarette butts, and everyone around us can smell it from a mile away.

And that seems to be the conundrum, the great debate between who we've always been and who we can always choose to be. We cannot outrun ourselves, nor can we leave behind what we have created; we must heal it first. Circumstances may change, people may come and go, and things are sure to come in and out of your life, as sure as the seasons bloom, but you will always be who you have designed yourself to be. You will always attract what you have designed yourself to attract. A change in environment, relationship, or business venture is only a temporary fix to the change you are really looking for. Baby, if you can make it right where you are, then you can make it anywhere. Your circumstances are only circumstances. The call on your life is bigger than your obstacles, and I urge you to believe in the things that aren't always seen.

When I stopped trying to run away from the pain, and turned around to look at it in the face, my acknowledgement alone began to cure the Dis-Ease.

My disclaimer is that creating a life where you can move forward, no longer afraid of pain, is going to take more than just believing. There's got to be an equal amount of work put in. The amount of work you put in, you will actually reap in faith and opportunity. You can believe all that you want, that a shiny unicorn is going to show up in the middle of the night and take away all your pain, with its sugar-white coat and long, flowing tail, but the reality of any transformation is that this is going to take some work. And the truth is, sometimes that work hurts.

It's going to require of you some elbow grease, some time on your hands and knees, and maybe even some tears. But when you've been the one working so hard for everyone else in your life, giving of yourself, trying to make relationships work, suddenly working on yourself becomes the easiest thing you've ever had to do. Giving yourself all the advice, all the love, and all the energy that you have been giving to everyone else, allows you to give even more from your stock. We cannot and should not give when our self-worth reserve is low. We must fill ourselves up and become whole. The achievement of wholeness is going to take some discipline, it is going to take some determination, and it's going to take a gentleness and ease in handling yourself. In order for you to ditch everything you have been, to make room for all the things in life you deserve, it's going to take some absolute drive and determination, a special piece for your mechanism to move, a secret sauce that can transcend the toughest of palettes, and all of this can be achieved through one of life's greatest gifts, our intention.

At first, I wondered what others would think of me. At times I felt discredited for the number of tears I poured into these pages. My hard copy was drenched, and my digital copy became exhausting to look at. I felt exposed, as if one day someone would find out all of my secrets. I felt fear in what I didn't know and what I wasn't taught. I wanted to be educated first, before I offered my gifts to the world, half-baked and full of discovery. And then I realized, it was through my discredit, it was though my lack of credentials, it was through my self-discovery and experiences that I was most qualified for the race I was preparing to run. Self-validation went through the roof when my 'what-if's' went out the window. Self-love became apparently clear when I looked through the eyes of forgiveness, to myself first, and then to others. And for the first time in a long time, I could see myself, standing there, beautiful for all that I had been through, all that I was, and truly beautiful for what I was becoming. However, all of my skills would have resulted in failed attempts, all the books I read would have fallen on deaf ears, and all the weight I lost was sure to return, if not for intention.

I have listened to some of the most amazing and highly successful people in the world, but once they finished speaking, without personal intention, their advice would simply go in one ear and out the other. Those areas that became blocks for me throughout my life, could not be moved by throwing books at them, listening to speeches, or even by bulldozing them with pretty dresses and makeup, because at the end of the day, there had to be a plan to take those walls down brick-by-brick.

And so, I built my intention in everything, brick-by-brick, until my walls of intention were higher than my walls of despair. I built my intention so high, I could climb up, stand on top of the fresh brick and mortar, then peer over the brigades that once had stopped me. I learned how to use my pain to my advantage, instead of falling victim to it. I learned how to stand on my story, and not in it. My field of vision expanded, and I became capable of seeing all the other possibilities that I didn't even know existed. I simply had to intentionally create the space to receive a better view.

Self-Love Edition

BREAKING BRAVELY

By: Stacie Winkfield

THE ADOPTION

Do yourself and others a service, know yourself. Therefore, when someone asks you who you are, you may speak in truth and authenticity.

I remember small clouded frames, like movie reels smothered in ash from smoke damage. Like someone threw bleach on my story, and the ink ran from the pages. My younger days are colored in tie-dye, and at times I wish I could remember more. Then at other times, I realize to not remember sometimes is a blessing. It is the body's natural way of protecting us from the things we are not ready to handle. It is like sedation, except the spirit provides the anesthesia and the mind the amnesiac effects. I can recall small moments, though. Moments in time that I allowed to shape the totality of my existence.

I was taking a bath with my younger sister, in a tub where all the porcelain had been eaten away. It was a dark, dingy bathroom, and I don't remember getting in the tub, just sitting there in comfort of the water. I always felt like the water was a safe place. A place where I could dip my head in just enough to cover my ears, and drown out the world around me. A small framed window over the sink was our only source of light. Mom was there, amongst a group of others gathered in the living room, laughing loudly. We were only there for a short period of time. It was a space in time, open long enough for a bath and a hot meal. These safe days were few and far between, for we were always on the run for our sanity and for our lives.

One night, I was dropped off at grandma's house. I remember getting a splinter in my foot from the wooden floor, and sitting on my grandmother's lap as she dug it out with a safety pin she heated over the fire on the gas-burning stove. That night, was my first encounter of sleeping in a bed with a cousin that I just met for the first time, but it would not be my last. The room was dark in the back of the house, with branches banging up against the window from the storm that night. And as I laid there, all I could think about was when my mother would come back and rescue me from yet another strange bed. The next morning, I was picked up by mom. Dragging my body like a sack of wet laundry down the street, I trotted with my small hand in hers. She took me to the adoption agency with my little sister and brother. And then suddenly, we were on the foster home "chitlin circuit," becoming the entertainment for different families one night at a time. Some of these homes were safe, and some of them were dark rooms and noisy chatter, with adult hands slipping under my purple cotton dress. But I still had my siblings, and since I was the oldest baby, I was determined to be strong for the younger ones.

The next time I saw grandma, we had a visitation at a train station, filled with the smell of coffee and nutty donuts. I hadn't seen mom for a long time, but when I did, her long brown hair was cut to the base of her neck, so she could no longer hide all the bruises or the shy, yet distorted look in her eyes. From that point on, with mom it was mostly more dark, small rooms. I was running and running, hitting, screaming, fighting, running and more running. A hand pulling down my tights at night at an age when I couldn't even understand why. Time to slip into the dark spaces of my mind. Foster homes with flashes of light and then no light. I lived in the dim and dingy. Constantly running with a heavy little heart and a tired spirit. I really couldn't even begin to tell you what the sky or the outside world looked like. My memory of that didn't even exist until I was adopted.

I can still see the florescent lights in the agency's ceiling above me, rectangular in shape, over the long wooden table. It was a white, sterile room with no pictures or flowers. There was nothing there to disturb you, and nothing to provide comfort. The waiting room had the same chairs with soft, gray cushions. A girl cousin of mine brought me peaches into this room, in a white Tupperware dish. Peaches must have been my favorite since she brought these for my parting gift. I didn't know what those peaches meant then, but the sweet juiciness somehow made me feel like everything was going to be all right. It was one of the first things given to me that I piled on top of all the emptiness I felt inside. My biological family was there, in one moment saying their goodbyes, and then gone the next. My little brother and sister were not there, and they would not be coming this time. This was the first place I can ever truly recall feeling left and alone.

It must've been around Easter Sunday, my caseworker, a brown, round, kind lady, gave me an Easter bunny with tall, smooth, milk chocolate ears. It stared back at me with its blue and white eyes along with other pink and yellow ornamentation. I never did get to taste that bunny. I wanted to bite into its buttons very much so, especially since I couldn't even remember ever getting a candy or chocolate up until that point, but it was taken away from me when I arrived at my new forever home.

To me, my new Mama was big on discipline, but now I know it was just her way of protecting me and trying to keep me safe. The chocolate bunny really would have been way too much sugar for a girl of my age, and in order to receive those monthly checks from the state, I had to be in pristine condition. I was angry, and so this is where the story I began to tell myself for so long, started. I made up in my mind, that she only adopted me for the checks she received. I was there to provide income for her family. The government sold me off; I was not selected. And so, my value came in the form of a dollar amount on a monthly statement.

I used to wonder in my four-year-old mind, how much children were worth in those days for adoption or foster care? For me, adoption was like being sold into slavery, then being expected to praise the slave master because she feeds you, gives you food, and provides you with shelter. But within my heart, I felt like a prisoner, unable to escape and run back home, unable to determine my destiny, and unable to see my mother's face. I looked for my biological mother, in any capacity, to come back and pick me up, but she never came to rescue me. Instead, she left me there, to save me.

My mother and I had one last visit after the adoption. She had been granted visitation rights, from what I was told. She could come see me if she wanted to, along with any other family members. She took me to a burger restaurant in downtown Flint, then across the street into a loft apartment where she was staying. There were a lot of people there too. She always did seem to have a lot of people around her. I remember the butterflies in my tummy, to see my mommy again. I wanted to get close to hug her, but she was busy taking a bath. I rushed into the bathroom when she called for me, and leaned over the side of the tub so far that I slipped and fell in, trying to run my small fingers through her wild, dark brown hair. I got my t-shirt soaking wet, and ended up having to wear an oversized adult shirt home, but none of that mattered. This was the last time I would see her face. My hamburger was eaten on the way home with raisin sun spilling into the windows of the vehicle onto my yellow, chubby cheeks. And when I got out of the car that day and waved goodbye, that would be the last time, the last hug with her that I would remember.

In the upcoming days, she became a close and distant memory. I never forgot her, but I forgot the intricacies of her face. I forgot her silhouette and how far my arms had to reach around her waist to touch the small of her petite back. My ears couldn't remember what my name sounded like in her voice, or what my voice sounded like calling out to her. I was angry. My new Mama, or ma'am, said even from the time I was a little girl, I had a slow, burning anger within the deepness of my big brown eyes, always shaking my foot erratically as I sat cross-legged, and she could never understand why. But I know why; I was angry at myself for forgetting.

There in my new home, I was expected to adjust and then to push forward, happily, ever after. But this house, the happy home that people thought I was looking for, I was never looking for. I was looking for my mother to get on her feet, to outrun the danger, and to hold me tight in her arms, saying that everything would be alright. So, for me, every day in my new home was only, the after. The after, of never again being a part of the only thing I had ever known. The after of living only with a couple pictures or memories of the sister and brother they separated from me. Was I supposed to just act as if they never existed? The after of dark, strange rooms, and the hunger in my belly that I had become accustomed to. Only, the after and I was expected to just "move on." But what happens when you can't just move on?

I came through the screen door of my new home and was told to sit on the floor next to the kitchen. In the beginning, I was overjoyed to be away from all the chaos. To be away from my siblings, and to have a space all of my own. I didn't know that space in which I was told to sit, would be my designated seat until I was seventeen years old.

Mama didn't care for the way I spoke to her. To her, it was considered rude and disrespectful. Mama was old-school, and ran her house and children as such. She had an older son and a daughter who were biologically her own. She always made it very clear to me, that she adopted me because she was concerned for my safety. She fostered me and my biological siblings in her home for a short period of time. And since my safety was her main concern, unfortunately us kids weren't raised with the same rules. She could only give me what she knew how to give me, up until that point. She didn't want to see me get hurt, and so she kept me locked up tight. I never minded the locks, but what bothered me the most was that the same rules didn't apply when it came to her own children. And so started the adjunct to my story, that she loved them more than she loved me.

I can recall having a couple options for how to address her. She said that I could either call her Ms. Winkfield, or say yes ma'am, no ma'am. I chose the latter since the first seemed too formal for the woman whom I wanted so badly to call mother, or mom. To say yes ma'am, no ma'am was admirable and considered good etiquette. I never felt weak for saying this or as if my power was taken away. What I did feel, was alienated and a disconnected from the family. Why was I the only one to use this language when her other children could call her Mama? No one I had known before was there to answer all the questions I had, or to help me navigate the circumstances. I didn't know what to say or not say. No one prepared me when I went into my new forever home, and I was left to figure it all out, alone. Until this day, I am still the only one of my siblings who says yes ma'am and no ma'am. Now it is something I pride myself on, but at that time my perception only meant one thing, distance.

For some reason, my biological brother and sister, who were both in foster care and had been fostered by Mama previously, could no longer stay. Somehow, they were taken back to the life we once knew. I considered them lucky for the longest time. You see, however dysfunctional our upbringing was, it was "our" dysfunction. And on the eve of every birthday that passed in the following years, I balled myself up in a fetal position on the floor of my bedroom and imagined a birthday card coming in the mail. When no one was looking, and it was just me, the darkness, and God, I wondered if that year would be the year of my mother's visit. I would cry out to God and wonder how I could have so many people around me, and still on the inside, feel so alone. I wondered, if there would be a present on the doorstep or a call to say how much she missed me. I even thought that one day maybe she would show up to take me back into the dark, dimness of the world in which we both previously existed. And inside I would ache for Dawn. That was her name.

I used to, and still think; it is by no coincidence that my mother's name was Dawn. Dawn; the first appearance of daylight; daybreak. Awakening and that's why my name is Stacie, meaning resurrection. Because within her awakening, was my resurrection. I was there with her since the beginning of time and throughout different levels of consciousness; I missed her so. I was angry because I was taken away from that of which I came. And that anger manifested into rebellion, an improper understanding of love, and a need to try to control the chaotic world around me.

As a child, I tied my identity to this one person. I felt that where I belonged was near the vessel from which I was created. I marinated in that young 12-year-old girl for nine whole months. My conception, a miracle, birthed from a place of destruction. I got drunk on the high cortisol levels flowing through my veins and arteries before I even arrived. I came to earth with her in the beginning, resurrected. I was carried by her mother and by the mother before her, renewed with each generation. The space was created in them, by God, for me. But sometimes when space is created, it is only made for us to be birthed through, not to stay complacent in. Space, in the time-space continuum of this reality, is needed for angels to be birthed through. But we could never experience the miracle for which they were created, if they chose to make their existence about that space and not about the journey after. How many of you are still holding on to your security blanket, blaming the results of your adult life on the residual's of your childhood?

It must have been a divine purpose for your existence, considering all the hell you had to go through to get here.

I became great at the imitation of life in the years to follow. I had no identity of my own, and through that lack of identity, I left my crawl space open and allowed the manifestation of abandonment to pour into and through me. From the beginning, I couldn't remember who I had been birthed to be amongst all of the chaos, therefore I abandoned myself. I tried to perfect the art of camouflage, and like a chameleon blend into the background of my surroundings. I tried to do my best to please Mama, but to no avail. I felt nothing I ever did was good enough. I continued to sit in the same place she made for me, day in and day out, next to the doorway of the kitchen, on the floor with my legs crossed, Indian-style. This was the only place in the house, where she was sure she could keep me within her eyesight at all times, and those eyes followed me through the home wherever I would go. When I asked permission to go the bathroom, when I would move over two feet to eat from my dinner plate seated on the kitchen floor, when I would stand in the corner for taking too long washing the dishes, I was always watched. Mama was watching me.

When we all gathered in her bedroom to sit and watch a family movie, I was not allowed to come all the way into the room. Sometimes, I was given permission to sit in the doorway, and I would attempt to fully see the screen from around the side corner of the wall. I was constantly put in a place, because she was scared that if I deviated from this place, I would end up like Dawn. And so, Mama kept a watchful eye and a stirring distance.

Sitting or standing in the doorways of my childhood home and never being able to go all the way through into the next room, followed me for years into my adult life. I became exhausted, trying to make myself smaller, quieter, drawing less attention, so I could be invited into the space that others left for me. Mama adopted another son when I was around seven years old, and I grew furious then, seeing my brothers lying on the bed beside her, eating potato chips and popcorn as I sat, watching from the sidelines. I felt forgotten. I've often noticed that in life, if people are given praise while working on a project, their engagement in getting a task accomplished increases. But Mama didn't hand out much praise; I received a seldom hug and never any kisses. She said that I wasn't allowed to sit on her bed, because I was adopted, and it was against state guidelines. So, I guess, no physical touch for that four-year-old little girl was the price I paid to be safe. The only physical touch that I received along the way, believing it to be love, was the touch from my father's and strangers' hands. And then there were the spankings in the palm of my hand for all the things I did wrong. Never praise for the things I did right. I was angry, I was furious, and that fury grew into rage. A rage that was explosive in my young adult years if I thought anyone was trying to hurt me anymore.

Space in the time-space continuum of this reality is needed for angels to be birthed, but we could never experience the miracle for which they were created, if they chose to make their lives about that space and not about the journey.

I felt ashamed of who and what I was and where I had come from. There was so much effort put into me "not becoming my mother," that I wasn't allowed to just be a little girl. But that little girl, who was all alone, who never felt good enough, who sat in the doorways of a home trying to simulate and become a part of the world that went on around her, grew up with the physical body of a woman and the spiritual body of a child. And so, my vision remained that of a child's throughout my young adult years. Large, but unenlightened; free, but without discipline; and wild, without regard to the unnaturalness of my internal turmoil. All of those feelings left unchecked and unbalanced, grew more and more stubborn, unfamiliar with what love truly looked like.

And then my picture board flickered, and Dawn was murdered.

At this point, any hope I carried in that small heart-space I held for her was lost, and I would no longer be able to see her face ever again. There was no need to cry anymore, she would not be coming. So, I stuffed the last bit of pain that lived in my body into the black pantyhose, dress, and Mary Janes I wore to her funeral. The hurt turned to numbness, like chronic pain. It was there, but I wasn't aware of the intensity of the discomfort. The ache in my body for my mother's presence was intense for so long I forget what it felt like. I grew to ignore it and function with its presence. There was no need to look forward to my escape from my new home anymore, the light in my dream was snuffed out and the only tears I had left, fell at the church where her body was held. The details of her murder were so graphic, the casket was closed. For the longest time afterward, I didn't feel, I didn't believe, I didn't hope, and I barely existed.

I felt truly alone and abandoned after my mother's death. The only fond memory I then had was one of my younger sister. She was only allowed to spend one night with me when I was around seven years old at my new home. For some reason, she needed a place to stay before she went to court the next morning. It was one of the few days during my childhood that I got to go outside and play, so I remember it well. Our neighbors made our yard an unsafe place to play unsupervised, so on most days, to keep us safe, Mama kept us indoors.

I remember my sister running around the back yard in circles, in a blue velour top and pink corduroy bottoms. Her hair was jet black and straight and reached the middle of her back. In the light of the sunset, she sang, so full of life, teaching me how to pop the heads off of the dandelions in the grass. I felt that day, as if God sent me a small gift to balance my inner suffering. In that moment, her presence was a distraction from all the lost years I spent without her. But this brief moment still would not suffice for all the emptiness left brewing inside.

My behavior during my teenage years was considered, by my Mama, to be disrespectful. I spent an enormous amount of energy, attempting to gain my mother's praise, and when I saw that the same attention she gave to my brothers was never going to be given to me, I gave up. My sister was away at college, and over breaks she'd come home to visit. Mama and her would get into arguments over me. My sister thought in some ways that I was being treated unfairly, and so my mother blamed me for being a wedge in their relationship. The arguing over me between the two of them made me feel hopeful and guilty all at the same time. Mama would always tell me that different children have different needs, and that everyone cannot be parented the same way. I actually agree with that statement now, even though I had to become a parent to understand this concept. I also understand now that all children need their mothers', "Good-job" and" You are enough." Back then, I held tight to the perception that Mama's love for the other kids was far greater than her love for me, because it didn't matter how many times I did the dishes or helped her clean her room when the boys were playing video games, or how late I stayed up helping clean the house, nothing I ever did or said resulted in more hugs or, "I love you." If I was ever so lucky, eventually she would grow tired and send me to my bedroom.

When I came home with all A's the first semester of school, this didn't get me promoted to a new seat in the house. I was still expected to do my homework in a dark-lit hallway, and could not go into my room because I wasn't afforded a light bulb. So, I gave up trying to keep good grades. I had always been smart; it never took much for me to get the content in books or apply concepts, but I no longer had a reason. The pain from feeling unwanted and not enough, at some point, grows into resentment. I grew resentful because I gave love but did not receive it in the way I felt I deserved. However, I stayed, because this had become my family, and no matter how dysfunctional it was, it was "our" dysfunction. I stayed until I turned 17 years old, and Mama sent an eviction notice to our address with my name on it.

At first, I was excited, to receive a letter. It was the first piece of mail I ever received that hadn't been opened before it got to me. I thought it was a sign that I was stepping into adulthood. I thought my mother was finally letting me have a little independence and would help me become a young woman. All of my behavioral issues, came from an inner feeling of lack, and a feeling that I could never be enough. No one ever told me I was enough, ever. It wasn't that Mama didn't love me, she just loved me the best way she knew how to, and I couldn't understand why she couldn't do better. When I asked if I could go to a movie with my friends or maybe call a friend on the telephone, or if I asked her for a ride to choir practice, she would dig in her heels to a firm "no," and I would dig in my heels to a firm, "doing it anyway." This push and pull resulted in a place in our relationship where she no longer could have me in her presence. I was not surprised when I opened the eviction letter, but I was heartbroken. I knew, even though we had a lot of ups and downs, that this was the new mother God had given to me so many years previously, and I loved her for all the things she had done for me, and even all the things undone. But now, here I was again, being forced to leave the only place I had grown to call my "home." Then I was back on the run for my life, alone, broken and forgotten. I never wanted to leave home. I was afraid, but I gave up all hopes of trying to stay. And so, I set out into my adult years with my own perceptions to guide me.

Change Your Story, Change Your Life

The story I told myself and others about my life in the past, the one you just read, was one version of the truth. It was a tale of sadness. I knew that when I told this story, I would attract looks of sympathy, like the "You poor thing, you really got a bad deal," kind of compassion. This sad tale was the only story I knew, and the only one I was willing to tell, until one day I got sick of telling it. I got sick of hearing my voice speak the words, like I was in a never-ending dress rehearsal for my own personal television series drama. I actually started to manifest physical symptoms in my body such as depression, back pain, and anxiety. At that point I knew I had to release all the stories that would not produce wellness in my life. Chronic pain is just spiritual pain unreleased and manifested in the flesh, an exacerbation of a life unfulfilled.

With intentional living and self-discovery, you can reshape the view of yourself and the world surrounding you. Life will become your oyster, your playground, so to speak. You will learn that we are not placed here to suffer, and there are no "bad deals." Every experience is meant to bring us to a higher level of consciousness and awareness. You and I have the power to change whatever way a circumstance affects us; it's all based on our perception of the experience.

Perception is one of the most powerful tools at the table of your heart, seated right next to choice. When I realized throughout my own life, that I had choice in every matter, everything changed and I no longer needed to drag my debilitating story with me like an old security blanket. I could now decipher and utilize my story for what it really was, a reference point to show people how far they can come from their perception of tragedy. Changing the perception of your story, can provide you with a quantum leap from the "woe is me" syndrome to a testimony, not as a lie but as an alternate version of the ultimate truth. No details that existed from my story have been changed or altered; I only created enough distance and space from the one version, so that I could see all the other possibilities. The more you focus on a particular incident, the closer and closer you get, and your vision of the event typically begins to get fuzzy. Out of the millions of possibilities that exist in any one situation, you get to interpret what you'll take away and what you'll give away. From that place you gain the armor to become the man or woman you've always wanted to be.

There are as many different possibilities as there are perceptions, and each person has the ability to create their own.

I know of two siblings who went from foster home to foster home in the early developmental stages of their lives. Sometimes, when placed in the care of their mother, there was no food, clothing, or safe environment available. The young girl and boy were both sexually assaulted on a consistent basis, for which they both received therapy for in later years. The occurrences of assault were so prevalent in these children's lives that when their mother had more children, the older siblings started to assault their younger brothers and sisters.

In their adult lives, the girl obtained some external validation of what most people would consider a "normal lifestyle." She attended and graduated from a prestigious university and traveled the world with her high-school sweetheart. She then went on to attend law school and became partner in a highly sought-after firm at a young age. Her husband is the love of her life, and they now have three beautiful children.

Her brother, in his experience, went on after high school to a correctional facility. He remains in prison for sexual misconduct. He always felt like he had no choice in the matter and gave up hope for change, telling himself that he would be institutionalized for the majority of his adult life.

I spoke with the children's aunt who assisted in raising them after the death of their mother. She says that she always hoped that things would change, once the abuse stopped, and once the boy was placed in a stable home, however, his conditioning did not allow him to overcome his addiction to seek love with alternative methods of affection. For him, he became a product of the story he was given and externalized that pain into the world around him.

Now I know very often, people ask themselves how can two children, who are raised in a similar environment, by the same parents, turn out completely different? The answer became inherently clear to me when I understood that each child is an individual, and therefore every child cannot be parented the same way. Every child will perceive one situation in a completely different way. It is the stories we tell ourselves about these events that shape our adult lives.

Be conscious of the choices you are making for yourself.

The story I used to tell myself, was that my birth mother didn't want me. I was unexpected and unwanted. Each birthday I would lie on the floor of my bedroom in a fetal position, sobbing uncontrollably, wondering why there was never a birthday card. I wondered why my birth family never bothered to call or send me best wishes. No one ever showed up, and I imagined that I simply was forgotten. I felt as if my presence as a little girl was insignificant. I must have been someone with so little impact within the hearts of my family that they could just go about their lives as if I never existed. I was begging for a pity-party. It was not until years later, I realized my beliefs were self-limiting and did not allow me to live the life of abundance I deserved.

The Shift

My children were getting ready for school one late winter day in Michigan. All morning I had wrestled with the idea of even attempting to transition into a new career. I finally settled into the, "What's the worst that could happen?" conversation with myself. As I looked into their happy, smiling, mischievous faces, I asked myself, a mother's worst fear, "What's the worst that could happen?"

Living a life of mediocrity and working for a company that no longer drove me to fulfill my greatest purpose was no longer an option, because I knew my kids needed a functional mother. They deserved a mother who could get out of bed and fix them a meal, someone to help close the smallest buttons at the nape of their necks. They needed a mother who I was completely incapable of being while drowning in my own self-sorrow. For me, there was no other choice than to change careers. It was a fight for my life, or running the risk of letting my own and my children's dreams die. They took their cues on sacrifice, sorrow, and dysfunction from me. And so, if changing careers is what gave me light, if that is what warmed my heart, if that is what made me a better woman for my three little girls, at that point, writing my book became all worth it.

So, I asked myself, "What's the worst that could happen?" I allowed my fear that paralyzed me for so long, to become the fuel to my fire. Asking yourself this very question will cause you to look at the facts concerning a situation and give them their proper perspective. Your mind might want to jump to the conclusion of the world as we know imploding and life as we know it ceasing to exist. But realistically, "What's the worst that could happen?"

Mentally, I started to take notes. OK, I could lose my job while writing my book because I was no longer willing to put in extra hours for someone else. I wanted to start putting all those extra hours in for myself. If I lost my job, I would then lose my apartment and have to go apply for government assistance, and maybe live from my car. I wouldn't have enough gas money to drive the kids to school every day or feed them, so they would need to go live with their father. And that was where my mental log ended.

Now I made up in my mind way before this moment, that losing my dream or serving other people wasn't the thing that scared me the most. It was the inability to care for my children, a mother's worst fear, because our first innate thought is one of self-sacrifice. It is to put our dreams on hold to secure their little hearts. The opposite of this is actually true, though. By putting our dreams on hold, we actually don't play our life like it's the final quarter, and therefore hold their hearts hostage. They sit, holding their breath, waiting for mommy to breathe so they can breathe. They are watching us, and it is your unspoken words, and all of your action dripping into them, hovering over their lives, that make them suspicious of your love. Someone once said, that it is important to find your purpose in life before finding your mate. How else are you to know who will be able to ride along throughout the journey with you? I would take it a step further and say it is most important to discover your purpose and live it before you have children. How can you teach a child to live the life of their dreams, if you're not leading by example?

Feelings of regret started to surface as I ran the mental images throughout my mind of dropping the girls off with their dad. Yes, I would still be able to see them. Yes, they would be well cared for, but to me it would indicate some level of failure on my part, and to me that meant letting them down. I realized that maybe my insignificance to my own birth family, was not what I thought it was. Maybe those same feelings of lack, regret, and failure kept them away for so long. Maybe, just maybe, they chose to make an unapologetic sacrifice, and instead of treating me poorly, ushered me into safety to build a life of my choosing.

To let a child, find its way in the world after it's 18th birthday, or into the arms of God after death, or into the arms of another family at birth is quite the opposite of failure. This release is at the mountain peak of unconditional love, because what we love most, we have to let go of. There in that place, within myself, with no other witnesses, my victim statement morphed from a caterpillar into a butterfly. My story changed from one of abandonment to one of unconditional love. My perception of what happened all those years ago was only one side of the story. Once I realized this, I was immediately healed.

People tend to do the best that they know how, or were taught up to that point. I gave myself the permission to change my story. Maybe my mother gave me away because she felt like it was the best decision for everyone involved. Whether it was or wasn't, I cannot continue to blame her for the outcome, something over which she had no control. The only control she had was in that initial decision, and that decision had to have come from a place of unconditional love. So, I began to thank my mother. I began to celebrate her. I began to praise that wisdom within her teenage mind.

To give a child that came from your body away, with the faith that he or she might have a fighting chance for survival and a secure environment, is unconditional love. In the Bible, it is the story of Moses, the story where a baby is released into the abyss of the unknown and trust is placed in the observer, unseen in life, to guide him along his way. That is a story of exemplary faith and courage. Once I recognized this courage, I was immediately healed. I changed my story, and by happenstance, life showed up and followed suit. Henceforth, the story I tell today is one of the greatest love stories of all times.

See, we could choose to look at the world head-on through binoculars, but we'd miss so much in our peripheral vision. We could also choose to gaze upon the world's events and circumstances through a kaleidoscope which might alter our picture, depending on the position in which our heads are tilted. Once love is the precipitating factor that drives your thinking, the heart and the mind begin to follow. It is possible to look at the world through rose-colored glasses, for once you are settled in your spirit, you can see darkness coming from a mile away. Our vision actually becomes more precise when we do not rely on our eyes independently to see. When you are not protecting yourself with physical strength, when you are not speaking from a place of learned language, you are able to open yourself up to be a conduit for the infinite to flow through. Infinite joy, infinite happiness, infinite wisdom, are all gifts ready to have a play date. It is our job to be as open as possible, for a funnel that is partially collapsed cannot receive everything life has to offer; it will eventually become clogged and start to backup. The funnel with a filter placed at the top of it's opening is so concerned with self-preservation and perceived dignity, that it not only blocks uncomfortable growth, it blocks waterfalls of vision and wisdom that normally are only delivered in bulk. I was never fearful of living a lie, until I became fearful of the life I was living based off the lies I told myself. I made the world so small and placed everyone and everything in a box, which resulted in being isolated, feeling misunderstood, and developing poor communication skills with those in the world around me.

Doing the Work

One exercise that works for a lot of my clients when attempting to change a perception is called "Box Work." I would like to do this exercise with you now. This is an external exercise, designed to reallocate the mental and emotional boxes we have placed people, places, and things in our lives that produce, to some extent, discomfort. This task is meant to broaden our perspective and enhance our awareness of our own control over how we feel about what happens in our lives. I remember telling my dad, that even though I knew mentally something was not good for me, it was still hard to control the emotion. He simply said, "Just change the way you feel about it." For me, this did not work; I could not just tell myself not to feel a certain way and then all of a sudden feel better. I have always been a hands-on learner and had to physically problem-solve.

For this exercise, you can utilize a jewelry box with multiple small drawers, a storage box with drawer compartments, or even a pack of post-it notes, if you'd like to place them in the shape of a box on your bathroom mirror. There are also the little dollar store boxes that are normally utilized for mints at wedding receptions and baby showers. The larger your realm of possibilities, of course, the more boxes you'll need.

I then want you to take something you haven't forgiven, or if you have forgiven, then something, anything that you wish didn't happen in your life. Maybe you're ashamed of this thing, or felt like if it hadn't happened, your life would have been better. Find that thing, within the story you tell yourself and others, and write it down. For example, "My husband left me and the kids for another woman." Say the thing out loud and write it down. Try to trace your life back to the time you felt a significant change in your ability to be free, when your perception of yourself or your gifts shifted, when you felt the abandonment and the discomfort of being left alone, and then call it up to the surface of your being.

I had to go back to when I was to three years old for mine. Whatever that thing is, "My mother left me because she didn't love me," "My boss fired me after 25 years of blood, sweat, and tears with the company," "My child is transgender, despite my best efforts to raise her to uphold good, Christian values." Whatever it is, call it up into existence, to where you can look at it face to face. I want you to say it out loud, and I want you to write it down.

Next, I would like you to take sticky notes or other sheets of scrap paper and write down at least six to twelve alternate endings to the story you've been telling yourself. Now at first, I don't want them all to make you feel good, I just want alternate possibilities. Let's aim for half and half. You start each sentence with the undeniable truth statement. For this example, let's stick with, "My husband left me and the kids." Now that is the truth, without tainting it, without twisting it, without placing blame. You are just stating facts.

Now if available, I want the very first ending you write down to be exactly what the person told you was the reason they destroyed your life, so to speak. If they have been so kind to give you this privileged information, kudos to them. This reason deserves a place in the sunshine, because at that moment it was their truth, even if you didn't believe it. So, if your husband stated, "I'm leaving this household because I'm not happy," write it down without changing a single word. If his reason was said, it exists and it is a possibility. It is always probable that when someone else does something that causes a disruption in your spirit, that it really has nothing to do with you personally. But since only saying brighter things is unrealistic, I want you simply to create some feel-good sticky notes and some nasty ones. Using your imagination is perfect, since you used it to make up your story in the first place.

After all possibilities are written out, I'd like you to place them in the boxes or the drawers, or if utilizing a mirror, you can place them in 4x4 or 6x6 blocks; whatever floats your boat. But, I prefer using boxes, which brings me to my next step. In every box with an alternate ending that makes the experience bring light into your life, I want you to place in that box a small token, sentimental in value, to give love and affection to yourself. One of your boxes may contain a small piece of dark chocolate, while you may spray the inside of another with your favorite perfume. Another box may hold an old black and white photo of you and your grandmother laughing, or a coin you picked up off the road while vacationing in Montego. Whatever it is that makes you feel good and brings up happy memories for you, put those things in the boxes that bring light. We will leave the other boxes with endings that cause you pain empty. In this way, you are not continually rewarding yourself for telling those sad stories. If you continue rewarding bad behavior, your life will remain as empty as those boxes.

If one of your alternate endings happens to be, "My husband left me and the kids, so our children could thrive with more peace in the house," and that makes you feel better, that deserves a treat. The token doesn't have to be expensive, we are building a relationship between the person you have always been and the one you wish to become, so it's more the thought that counts.

At the start of each morning, I'd love for you to go to your boxes and begin stating aloud to yourself, in a mirror your personal truth, for example, "My husband left me and the kids" and then I want you choose a box you'd like to live for that day. You choose the story in which you'd like to tell. In this way you get to choose to live, that alternate truth. You also get to celebrate with yourself daily with little, just-thinking-of-you gifts for happy endings. Bonus!

We must fill ourselves up with love first before we can love others or expect love in return. Those boxes that hold special things of value are self-loving instead of self-sabotaging. You celebrate a shift into a new level of consciousness and a new way of being. You take control of how you react to every situation in your life. You no longer internalize or take accountability for other people's choices. Eventually, you can start replacing, one box at a time, the old beliefs, until all of your boxes are only filled with things that speak light into your being. Soon you will come to a day where all of your boxes are transformed and only contain positive sayings that propel you forward.

This exercise will not be for everyone. Some people may look at your boxes and call you crazy, and that's okay. What works for you may not work for them. This exercise is for those of you who need a little more hands-on learning; it's a small way to dedicate a consistent time for you to reach into, explore, and exploit how much bigger, greater, and open your possibilities are. I want you to carry that possibility with you. Some days, you may pick a different alternative, and that's okay, because every one of them can be true, even all at the same time. When the next person asks you, why your husband left, then "insert new story here," one that builds character onto your well-being.

HEAL YOUR WOUNDS THROUGH SELF-LOVE

We are seriously raising babies here, when dealing with issues of abandonment that may have initiated during gestation. When a newborn comes into this world, it is admired and gazed upon with such awe. There is usually an infinite amount of love that surfaces, that you may have never even known existed, previous to the arrival. There is a vast amount of patience we exhibit as we learn about the developmental stages of the baby, through the toddler and school-age years as well. We are excited when our little bundle of joy takes its first steps, gets its first tooth, and finally poops in the potty. These steps give us a sense of accomplishment. Never again in life will we ever be this euphoric over seeing poop! Clearly, we are in love, wiping their snot on our sleeves, placing the soles of their shoes above our knees to tie them, taking on the wounds of pregnancy with stretch marks, insomnia, and some occasional urinary incontinence. We know that "in love" requires a special kind of patience, kindness, and endurance.

What helped me and a lot of others I've spoken with, when dealing with feelings of abandonment, is to over-conceptualize the child left inside us that still hurts. We take our deficit in spirit, the hole deep inside, the hurt child, and we learn how to care for it, as if it was external of us. Whatever the initial event that caused the hole, deficit, or hurt, the offense done to us does not matter. How we respond to the event, and take care of ourselves within the face of uncertainty however means everything.

Thinking of ourselves as a mother, a wife, or an employer puts us often in the position of caregiver, in which others rely on us to provide safety, security, and stability. We can still remain in these roles while adding another being to the top of the list of our priorities. The thing is, you must know that this person is of the utmost importance, because if his or her needs aren't met, then the whole play called life, ends in shambles, with not enough time, broken promises, tiring days that no amount of sleep can cure, emptiness, and a lack of love for life that often feels like death.

The one person, numero uno, you have to place at the top of your list is the baby version of yourself. As adults, we have to learn how to parent, love, and show compassion to ourselves. We have to take care of the baby in our spirit. Our inner child has always been present and will always be present, but if not taken care of, supervised, or disciplined, it can show up in our adult lives, sabotaging good feelings and meaningful relationships.

When I started to love little, baby Stacie as an external entity, I had fewer feelings of anxiety. There was a comfort there that I provided for myself, so I no longer required external things, places, and people to validate my happiness.

Talk to yourself, and yes, it's okay if you answer back. Talk to yourself as you would your child, after all we are all but children, walking around in taller bodies. I understand that some of you may have a difficult time parenting others; you may have difficulty valuing a human life and may have to place your caring skills into yourself as you would an inanimate object or maybe a fur friend. Whatever the object of your affection may be, I want you to love yourself as you love that thing. Maybe it is a childhood toy, or a fancy brand-new car, but whatever the object is, I want you to desire yourself more than anything in the world. That love, that care, and all that attention that may be placed in your music, your fitness, or your money; give yourself permission to give and receive it within yourself.

A friend of mine, let's just call her Mindy, was preparing to enter a specialty grocery store outside of the town in which she lived. She had driven into the city earlier that morning to see a client. This one particular grocery store was one that she loved because it was an advocate for farm-to-table produce and sold a variety of whole foods. There were beautiful fresh flowers inside, freshly ground spices, and the grocer still asked, "Paper or plastic?"

Paper or plastic was like music to Mindy's ears in a new digitalized generation where everything was readily accessible at the swipe of a button. She was often at home and comforted within the familiar. She loved this store, but had only visited it once before. Her boyfriend knew how much she wanted to go there, and how much she admired the store owner's mission statement and company values. So, on the eve of the day he proposed, they went there together. Searching through endless aisles of organic dairy and good Michigan-grown cherry wine. For

Mindy, it was the equivalent of a midday gift from the gods. And the setting made one of the most perfect days of her life, even more perfect.

But on this day, she sat there in the parking lot, in the driver's seat of her car trembling. Passers-by went about their lives effortlessly and carefree, but not Mindy. She sat there, paralyzed. This one building amongst the millions of four-walled, upright structures in all the world, held a significant amount of importance in her life. The break-up between Mindy and her now ex-fiancé was the memory of her breaking her own heart. She loved this man very deeply, and wanted the arguing in the relationship to stop. But she knew that if they were to marry at that time, it would be a sacrifice to her purpose. So, as painful as it was, Mindy called off her engagement. And as she sat at the storefront of where it all began, all she could do was cry tears of regret. She sat there, wondering if the choice she made was the right one. And now every special place they once visited, would now have to be revisited on her own.

It is amazing sometimes, how we give so much of our own power over to buildings and mementos and people, whose only commitment is to themselves. Mindy was terrified to walk through the rain and up to the door, to step in amongst the people, alone. She started to panic, wondering if she would ever find the love of her life. Her fiancé had since moved on, started dating another woman, and even took his new girlfriend to the same places he had taken Mindy. Here he was, dancing all over the memories of their relationship, in and out of town, but Mindy couldn't bring herself to open the door of the car.

If you have ever had a child who was afraid of the dark, or maybe one who believed that there were monsters under the bed and they'd start to cry, what would your reaction be? In my home growing up, it didn't matter if I cried; I was not comforted. I was to accept the fear and move on with my life like everyone else. There was no night-light, but there were night terrors. There were no hugs, or kisses, not even an "It's going to be okay." Mama's solution was to keep me up longer at night so that I was "too tired" to be bothered with my discomfort. The real cure came, when I realized it was okay to love me, not only to love me but to tell that child inside, still afraid, still hurting, still alone, that everything was going to be okay. I had to stop looking for people external of me to give me the things that I needed to give to myself. So hug yourself, tell yourself it's going to be okay, tell yourself, "Good job." All that self-love is worth it.

How many of us treat our children, as well as our inner child, the way our parents treated us? When a child starts to cry, whether it's going into a store, going with a stranger, or their feelings are just hurt, what do you tell your child? Do you tell them to "shut up," forcing their small wrists in the store? Do you spank them, in an attempt to "beat the fear out?" Did you know that the same gentleness and ease you give to your child during stressful situations is actually a mirror reflection of the gentleness and ease you give to yourself? What is the loving response you offer to yourself in the midst of anxiety and fear? Do you even know what a loving response is?

Mindy attracted people in her life that did not know how to be there for her, because she had not been taught how to be there for herself. In this moment, the easiest choice would have been for her to simply drive off and go to a different store. Another empty, but temporary band-aid would be to force herself to go in the store, but what good ever comes from exerting power and trying to force things? Even if you have the power to do so, who wants to live that way? And who benefits when you make someone do something they really don't want to do, even if that someone is yourself?

Instead, Mindy took a time-out for herself. She sat there in the car and hugged herself tightly. She told herself, aloud, that everything was going to be alright. She began to rock with herself, or I should say, rock with her inner child. She said to her child, "I will stay here as long as you need me, we are going to get through this together."

Within this moment, she no longer needed anyone else. There was no one she could call that could fix the job she had to complete on the inside. She made a commitment to be there for herself when no one else was, even when they promised to be. The only promises she knew she would be able to count on, were the ones she made to herself. She hugged herself tight, she cried, she watched a meditation video online, and there in the car, sat with herself and her inner child for the next 30 minutes.

The panicked feeling that overcame her physical body did not disseminate completely, but it became manageable. It is my belief, that this feeling is what we all want within those deepest moments of despair. If only the pain could be tolerable. It is easier to have pain that comes and goes, rather than deal with constant discomfort. We don't want the pain to consume us or to debilitate us to the point in which we cannot function. We just want it not to be the first thing we think about when we wake up in the morning, and the last thing we think about before we go to sleep at night. At least when we sleep, let us not dream about it. Let us at the very least, get a good night's sleep, and not be restless, in which we have to keep waking up from the tortuous thoughts that haunt us on a completely different level of consciousness, right?

Learning how to care for the child left inside and behind, hurting and in pain, acting up and lashing out, helps us to discover our capacity to love. Caring opens up the door to a newly found friend, your best friend. This door opens up a new love for a new being with ourselves. I always tell my closest friends and clients to remember, "we are raising babies here," and those babies are us.

Be Kind to and Easy with Yourself Like a Father

I believe one of the best types of love is a father's love. There is no ill will, there is providence. There is no competition, there is giving you of the best to get you to where you need to be. There is sacrifice, and above all wanting to see the child happy. This is why I believe a relationship with God is the most important to have for any man or woman. For this relationship is the way by which a man is taught how to be a man, and a woman is taught to receive love from a man. A woman cannot teach a man how to be a man, a woman can only teach an idea. For a woman, you will marry your father. And just to be clear, I don't believe in daddy-less daughters, I believe we tend to focus on the wrong "daddy." Look to love yourself, As the Father loves you.

The relationship between a child and her dad is the one in which she learns what to look for in a mate. There are no homeless children spiritually, just girls and boys who have forgotten how to get back home. You are being kept by the Lord, and so it is not that easy to get to you, for to get to you, they must pass by the way of your Father. And if they make it close to you, He allowed them to, to teach you a lesson or grow you up.

As a single person, it is important to live a whole life. I build myself up through my own accomplishments and need no external stimuli to inflate my ego. When I achieve a goal, I know it is the Father that helped me to achieve it, and so I thank Him. I am so grateful for His presence and how

He keeps me. He provides me with financial support to cover all of my needs and most of my wants. He provides me with shelter and clothes on my back. He provides a safe environment for my children and nourishment, wisdom, bedtime stories and blankets to cover their little faces. He provides spiritual nurturing and a place of unconditional love. I am kept, and to ask for my hand, you must ask the Father.

Therefore, it becomes easy to guard my heart, because in order to get close to me, you have to at least provide me with what my Father provides for me. He is my example for how a man is supposed to treat me. Now, I know we are not perfect and we are not God, but the man must follow the guidelines, walk in His footsteps, and reside his heart in the house beside the voice of truth. Nothing comes by me, that is not of my Father.

Simply put, I can provide for myself. If I'd like to go to dinner and a movie, I can take myself. I can go to the carnival or zip-lining or shopping alone. I have abundance in every area of my life. My girls are very well-cared for and bursting in spirit and life at the seams. So, what i'm trying to say is, that it's going to take some convincing for me to accept a man in my life. What I am asking is, what exactly does he bring to the table?

Be Single, In and On Purpose

One of my biggest aspirations in life used to be to get married. I'm only candid with this information, because I believe there are lot of women that have settled into a situation because they have given up hope of the ideal partner. But you are the ideal partner, just not for everybody. And when we grow in discernment, we can recognize when its time to exit a situation going nowhere fast, and truly have a field day.

I grew up in a household where soap operas were on every day for at least two to three hours. Since we didn't go outside much to play and there was no partner for my mother in the household, soap operas became all the media I received to show how relationships should work. The people involved in the scenes were always on guard. We couldn't wait until after they came back from a commercial break to see the end results of things gone wrong. Who would cheat on who next, while suffering from an identity crisis, creating a baby out of wedlock, and then trying to cover it up? Yes, soap operas sang the tune of dysfunction into our hearts. I never could quite pinpoint when the dysfunction became a generational addiction for stay at home moms. But I can't even tell you for how many hours, day in and day out, millions of people stayed home to tune in. There was a target audience, a core demographic, who lived to watch the of pain of someone else's life, with a couple of scattered joyous occasions. The life they lived for was riddled with drama. Drama makes for good television, but causes disassociation with the reality of life happening around us, every day. So now, I'm very careful about what I allow myself and my children to watch. You mustn't only guard your heart, but your eyes and your ears.

Since there was no "man of the house" growing up, I yearned to have that male energy present that would love me the same as my mother. Each of us are born having to navigate through the female and male energy, identity, and pieces of ourselves. It is important to have someone who has been there before, present to guide you through putting together the pieces. When one of those energies is missing from the picture, it is easy to get deterred from a clear picture of who we are. So, we walk into young adulthood with a lopsided view of how the world works.

All the things I was given were always ever so clear, but what of the things I didn't receive? I learned how to become independent and self-reliant, how to survive, and how to get what I wanted by any means necessary. I learned not to let anyone disrespect or disrupt my being in the obvious ways, like physical abuse. But that was the basis of what I acquired, survival. I struggled with how to be an effective communicator, how to trust people and to trust myself, and didn't even know what it meant to give and receive love. Because where I came from, "what's yours was mine, and what's mine was mine."

The giving and receiving of love was hard to attain even from my mother, and through the colored screen within a television box, it was all an act. I had no idea what real love looked like. My subconscious mind, predominately played out most of my relationships as a young lady in the manner I saw on the screen, except I didn't attract all the wealth of the soap operas, only the drama.

I was told to get married young while I was still beautiful, as if later in life my options would decrease, or that youth and prettiness were enough to carry me over the alter. Youth and prettiness can get you carried over the altar, but you also will have to depend on that to sustain whoever is doing the carrying. To be single is one thing, but to be single with kids has its own stigma attached by men and women alike. Time is of the essence, we say. "Well, you ain't getting no younger," was a comment I heard all the time, but it came to a point where I chose myself instead of choosing marriage. I realized I wasn't choosing the person, I was choosing the idea that my mother wanted for me. I see so many women walking around in dysfunction, unhappy, overweight, unfulfilled, and under-appreciated, following a man who cannot lead them spiritually, thinking that their relationship with God, will cover them both. One thing that they can all do is hold that left hand in the air like a badge of honor because indeed they had someone "choose" them. News flash ladies, you can choose yourself!

I'm Married Now, but at What Cost?

After the father of my three girls and I separated, I was mortified. I thought to myself, not only am I in my early 30's, but who is going to want to marry me with three kids? I know I can't be the only woman in the world who ever had this thought. Or maybe you thought that you might have to settle because you look at your children as baggage. Your children are not baggage, they are a bonus! After I broke it off with my children's father, every single man I dated was single, had no children of their own, no ex-wives hiding in the bushes, and perceivably no baggage. How was I going to find someone to love me, stretch marks and all? Who would put their happy, detour-free life on hold to pack school lunches and change diapers? Dropping off the girls at school and keeping a booster seat on deck is not the sexiest thing to do on a morning that you would have normally slept in. And then I met many men who were up for the challenge, and it became a huge measure for them to love my children, but not my only criteria. I shifted into a place where I wanted more as a woman.

During this time, I realized that getting married was still an option for even me. Not only was it an option, but I could have someone who was handsome and had integrity. I was worthy to receive someone I could trust, who treated me like a lady. I indeed was blessed enough to have someone to support me and my girls and everything changed. Everything or at least almost everything I wanted in a relationship was still an option, I just had to believe it. See, if you don't believe in something, then that option won't exist for you. So, ask yourself, what are the things you believe to be possible for yourself?

My thoughts shifted, and I began to think, whether a man would be what I wanted for me and my children. I no longer felt the need to settle down, I was living to level up.

I remember waking up one morning at my fiancé's house. He was a man whom I really loved deeply and thought we would be a witness to each other's lives until the next. Just a note: you don't need a man to be a witness of your life; there are millions waiting to see what you have to offer. I always felt safe in his presence and he was as honest as he could be. The way he looked at me, I could tell he loved me, but love wasn't enough, and I wanted more from a life partner. I laid there awake, in his bed, watching his chest rise and fall and listening to the incoming and outgoing breath escaping his lips. I even traced the outline of his lips with the tip of my index finger. He was a great friend, kind-hearted, and completely out of touch with the broken home from which he came from.

As I surveyed the room before me, I realized I was on an "island of dysfunction." Sometimes the bed can seem like a sanctuary. Somewhere the both of you can come together at the end of a hard day to energize each other and create your own rules and laugh at your inside jokes. The bed can turn into a place of imagination and play where the wild things roam. But are you going there to recharge and come out, or are you going there to hide from the world that greets you as soon as your big toe touches the floor? If you are not intentional in your reasons for being in the bed, you can actually have some moderate to severe discomfort in your life, once you get out of the bed. Have you ever wondered why most depressed people just want to sleep? They wish that when they wake up all of their troubles will be a thing of the past. Who are you once your feet hit the floor? Do you hit the floor running, or do you hit the snooze button every five minutes?

My fiancé's bed was made, but his spirit was messy. His "room" was dirty and there was not enough space for me. I didn't realize it then, but you must be careful of how people present themselves and their environment to you, because what is going on outside is also going on inside. We often choose to turn a blind eye to things that don't push us to be greater because we are comfortable. So I ask you, who pushes who when both of you bask in comfort? If there is one of many things I know, sometimes the truth is uncomfortable, and sometimes to love means letting go.

Now, don't worry, my mother still finds every opportunity she gets to explain to me how I missed out on a "good" man. But the question I ask of myself will be the same question I ask of you. Do you want a good man or do you want a great man? Do you want a good man, or a phenomenal one? Do you want to try to lead your husband to Christ or do you want someone who can lead and grow you? Do you want someone who shows up at graduations, or someone who is there when the children ask, "When is daddy coming home?" What is it that you want? This "Good Man" syndrome is killing us! We don't have any idea that there is a lack of money, but we have been conditioned to believe there is a lack of men. Any time your intention comes from a place of lack in relationships, you will accept less than desirable candidates. Either we don't believe the type of man we want really exists, or we don't believe we deserve the type of man we want!

Are you attempting to fill a hole from the outside-in, so much that anyone is better than no one? Our perceptions, or maybe even our mothers' or their mothers' perceptions have driven us to believe that to be alone is to be lonely. To be alone, to be single is seen as unbearable to most, and in some places, may not even be socially or culturally acceptable. So, we reach out for the new "fix" of the 21st century, the highest high, the power pill that will make us appear to be limitless, a relationship. Then when our idea of relationship romanticizes itself into a situation-ship we jump from person to person to measure our worth against those around us. For this reason, I am single, "On Purpose." Momentarily, I'd like to love on myself a little bit longer.

Too often, we give away so much of ourselves. We are pulled in so many directions, that every day becomes a default, instead of an action on the way to your breakthrough. Becoming aware of my higher level of consciousness made the significant and insignificant all the same. I simply began to trust the path and flow of my life. I knew that whatever I wanted for would be provided. Whenever I wanted to call anything into existence, it already existed. I didn't even have to open my mouth, for the most power is heard in silence. The heart is where my intention started, and it ended in my mind when I let go of the need to know the end result. How everything was going to work out became absolutely none of my business. My attitude and my servitude became everything.

Every day without action towards breaking the glass ceiling I hung above my personal dreamland, was as painful as a long-term disability, and if I allowed it to sit there long enough, it would have become a long-term disability. But I am not disabled; I am passionate for life and cannot sit back and allow myself to die slowly. Sometimes, I think this inaction is the very reason people love things that are not always the healthiest spiritually, physically, or mentally. Deep down, when you are not playing full out in all the key areas of your life, it is like a slow death. It can feel like hell on earth to live in a mundane space, so people hold fast to the thought of a better place. We commit spiritual suicide, hoping to find our better place more quickly. This mediocrity is the way that people kill themselves slowly without it being radically recognizable.

The process is more subtle than slitting your wrist in the tub or swallowing a bottle of pills. We don't want all the major red flags to go up, we want to get away with killing ourselves without the world taking notice. Heroine, now that's a no-no, but a couple cigarettes a day, and ah, much better. That's only a small batch of poison people don't care to recognize anymore. Food might be your small batch, or complacency, autopilot relationships, even the career that literally "makes you sick" can be your batch of poison.

Make This Your "Better Place"

Action was so needed in my life that it became the thing I would die for. The goals I set for myself became so unrealistic, that only then could I become the work I wanted to be. Don't do the work, become the work. My purpose walked side by side with me in the park, holding my hand when I got lonely. My purpose took hold of my shoulders and kissed me goodnight on my forehead. My purpose made everything all right and worth living. One thing I could depend on is that it would never abandon me, and that what I put in I was destined to get out. So, once I reached the point where my gift became laser-focused, I would not let anything or anyone stand in the way of my beaming light. I refused a realignment, a redirection, or a so-called short cut to the finish line. I knew that the race

God trusted me with, I could not trust in the hands of others. My purpose was something I had to complete on my own before inviting others to the after-party, and I had to be prepared first. I got lost in my purpose. I became conscious of my purpose. I became single, "on purpose."

WHAT MAKES YOU SPECIAL

What makes you unique makes you special. There is no one else on this planet better at being you. Isn't God magnificent?

Keeping what makes you special is not as easy as it sounds. Sometimes you can logically know all truth to overcome emotion, and at other times, your ego or inner child can produce a visceral pain so intense that you willingly hand yourself over to another person and commit spiritual suicide.

I knew it was the end of me and my fiancé's relationship, the man I badgered into proposing, when we were sitting in the pastor's office receiving pre-marital counseling. Even though the rhetoric of counseling in this situation was in regard to Christian principles based on the Bible, the universal truths remain unchanged across all religions, all nationalities, all creeds, and all versions of spirituality.

The pastor referred to a text, stating that all women are looking for a man that can lead them spiritually. He then went on to say, that this leadership is why some women fall in love with the pastor or fall in love with God so passionately, and their husbands don't want them going to church. The man has a spiritual deficit and has to relinquish control over to another power to reign over his wife in that area of his life. Now, I think it's good to be in love with God and the god or goddess within yourself, however I could not imagine trusting this man that sat across from me to lead me spiritually. I mean, while I was searching for something to bring my soul into a higher state of consciousness, he was at home "catching up on sleep." My children and I were at church, but the seat beside me was empty. At times, I hoped he would come through the door at the last minute and show up for our relationship, but he did not.

The pastor stated that the man is supposed to be the head of the household. That if a marriage fails, it is the man's responsibility, for the husband answers to God on the behalf of his family. Now this does not mean that the wife cannot turn to God and build a foundation of protection for her family and life in prayer, but still the spiritual body of marriage, as I understood it from this pastor's standpoint, was a hierarchy in which there was God, then my husband, then myself, and then my children. So, this meant to me, that on behalf of myself and my children, this man would speak to God on behalf of our protection, on behalf of our growth, and on behalf of our abundance in life. At that point, I agreed with my fiancé, I did not trust him. Not trust in the sense that he was a liar, but I didn't trust in his ability to lead our family. I think a lot of women get into trouble thinking that their spirituality is more than enough for them and their spouse, and then someone with less spiritual awareness is given the authority to become the messenger and the receiver between themselves and the source. I knew I preferred a direct connect.

Often times we tend to bond to the brokenness within one another. Especially as women, we want to be the nurturer of the man, and when a man is in love, he wants to be the nurturer of his woman. We fall in love based off of circumstances, instead of love. Men will search for a woman to lead them spiritually, and this can throw off the balance of male and female energy.

For the mate of your choosing, look for God to show them their purpose and lead them along their own path of spirituality before finding you. Your interaction with a partner is to teach within the experience of relationship, but both people must be whole in order to learn and grow from one another.

When the day comes, when I am to choose a husband, that person must be a teacher, a believer, and comfortable standing in the presence of greatness.

Determine What Are Your Unique Gifts, What Are Your Super Powers

Now if another being wants to enjoy the experience of your unique gifts, it is equally important for them to know their own. How else can they determine what they have to offer?

Asking yourself what your unique gifts are by doing some inner work is extremely important, so that when outside forces come to persuade you into something that you are not, your awareness of who you are takes precedent. For example, learning to trust myself was one of my biggest challenges. When people said that not trusting others was a sign of not trusting myself, I became frustrated and confused. How could it be, that if someone cheated on me, it was my fault? I mean, I trusted myself not to date anyone else or see someone outside of the relationship, so where was the lack of trust on my part?

I dated a guy who did all the things that I appreciated, who I believed, at the time, could have been a potential life partner. This man did not exhibit every single characteristic that I wanted, but at first, I considered our meet-ups as just "having fun," so it didn't concern me much. I knew from the beginning we were not meant for each other, since I am a "feeling" person, but due boredom, we continued to date.

As time went on, I really began to adore all the time we experienced together, but still could not understand why there was no connection. Why hadn't my heart opened up? He invited my children and I different places, always treated us kindly, made plans at least four or five days in advance, and called several times every day. So, what was the issue my gut feeling was telling me to watch out for? He knew that one of my love languages was gift giving, so every time we met he would bring small but meaningful tokens of affection. He lived an hour away and would drive with enthusiasm just to assist me with taking my mother grocery shopping, and then thank me for inviting him. Clearly this man loved me, right?

Well, at least he said he did. In imaginary world, in the back of coffee shops we discussed future plans of what could be ahead for us down the road. I met his parents, he fueled my car, he was perfect. Or was he? I sat and debated with myself, and then talked to God to determine what the heaviness in my chest was about. One thing that I was so pleased with is that in this relationship, I never stuffed my spark in a drawer or became smaller to fit in his space. I was unapologetically authentic at all times, vulnerable, and open to the possibility of true love.

However, there was this feeling, and after quite some time of searching within myself to see what the emotion meant, what my inner child was trying to tell me, and what I knew from the beginning was that, I didn't trust him. I had to say those words out loud in my office at work, and then it dawned on me what all of my feelings meant.

"I don't trust him?" Well, what kind of sense did that make? Was this my instinct, that thing called a "gut feeling" my mom always told me about? In order to avoid self-sabotage, which can become present when we start to experience a love that we are not used to or feel like we don't deserve,

I went to prayer to request confirmation. At the most fundamental base of your intimate spiritual relationship with the source is guidance. You have the ability to ask for what you want, believe it, and receive it. At this point, I suppressed my panic and anxiety, and the urge to call and break things off. At the same time, I gave space between myself and the need of his presence in my life. I became an observer and a lover, meaning I began watching him closely but allowed myself to move forward in our relationship. I opened my heart with discernment, because if he was "the One," nothing could stop God's intervention on my life.

There was this beautiful man with all these wonderful characteristics that made me warm inside, but I also paid keen attention to the things I didn't like. Sometimes, in the midst of love, we look for all the good in one another, but there are faults that are always present from the beginning. You just have to be willing to see them. Now, I didn't pay a considerable amount of attention to the faults, just the same amount that I applied to all his nobilities. I became balanced in my judgment, and there surfaced a few things that didn't coincide with what I wanted my life to be a part of. I considered looking past those faults, because like you, I told myself, "No one is perfect," everyone is human, and therefore everyone will have faults. But just because everyone will have some sort of fault, does not mean you have to deal with them all.

I took the feeling, burning deep in my stomach, a step further and consciously made a choice to ignore my inner warning signal and to love him freely, but with boundaries. Do you know what? God still showed up because I asked. In that office on that day, not only did I decide to ask what my emotion of distrust meant, I made a choice to receive the news and take action, whether it was good or bad, whether I liked the answer or not.

If I asked some of you reading to raise your hand for every time you looked for a truth, prayed for a yes, but ignored it, crying and throwing temper tantrums, when it came through as a no, some of you would have to do the hokey-pokey and put two hands in, then two legs, two arms, two feet, your nose, your head, and whatever other body part you could afford.

I already knew what my answer was anyway. How many of us could raise a hand, about asking God a question that we already knew the answer to? But let's not call it a test; let's just refer to it as going to prayer for confirmation. I knew the answer when I said a prayer of gratitude over my meal, and he would look at me in admiration, hold my hand, but never utter a word of his own. I knew when we went to church together, but he was agnostic and could not wait to get back outside the doors. I knew we did not share some core beliefs. So, you're probably wondering just what happened when God showed up, and how He showed up.

There was an old friend of his visiting from out of town that happened to be in town the same night I went to prayer, open to the possibility of understanding. She was a female friend that my current love interest told me two weeks prior would be coming to see him. He explained, that he promised her before we met, that he would join her in outings around the town to catch up on old times with mutual friends. He had asked me if I was okay with him keeping these plans.

One thing about really knowing your worth and loving yourself is that you know the extent of the creator's love from which you came. In knowing that love you also come to know that everything that is created for you is only for you. Your blessings have your name on them! So yes, I told him to go have fun with his friends, because no one can take from you what is truly yours. And sometimes, this is where you receive confirmation, not in trying to control what others do, but by standing firm in your own love of knowing who you are and where you come from.

When he came to see me that Friday night, the first night he was scheduled to go out with his old friends, he had a fresh haircut. Ladies and gents, I want to be clear on something here, a behavior so slight it may almost be missed. If someone drastically changes something about themselves, it is my belief that it is for one of the three following reasons. Radical change is either for themselves, someone else, or for you. Either they are growing to improve and make themselves feel good, or they are trying to impress someone else, and you have a 50/50 chance of it not being about you at that point. If you compliment the changed behavior, look, or action and get a lack-luster response, this is your Warning. The change is not for you, do not read into it, do not pass go, do not collect $200!

When I complimented him on his fresh haircut, he responded as if it never happened, and he played it off as if it was nothing. We had a good time together while he was in my presence, but his attention was elsewhere. It took him quite a bit of time, effort, and reflection to answer questions, as if his mind was preoccupied.

That night, he left and went out with his friends. He made plans to come spend time with me and the children the next day to make up for lost time. I agreed to accept his previous relationships that were intact before ours, because he stated there was no romantic interest. I've learned to trust other people to be simply who they are and not who I want them to be. His reason for not inviting me was placed on the fact that I had children, and he knew I wouldn't want to be away from them for too long, even though we previously had gone out while my oldest daughter babysat. He also explained to me that he told his female friend all about me, that we were dating, and that she was happy for him. His reason for not inviting me had nothing to do with the fact that I had children. The underbelly, the hidden agenda was to not have me present for his purpose alone.

The next morning, I "felt" the life-force change between us. His pattern of communication became disrupted, and he also didn't keep his word to come to spend time with the kids and me. His paradigm had shifted. We were no longer in the place that we once were. The plates in the earth as I knew it shifted the foundation of the house that our relationship was built on, and I had to then make a choice of whether I was comfortable after the quake had subsided. I felt this shift, and I did not ignore the uneasiness within me. That feeling I had was the gift of intuition. I finally realized why I didn't trust him, because from the beginning I didn't trust my own intuition.

The gentleman was kind enough to explain to me, after various moments of deception and making me feel like I had trust issues, that he and the other girl ended up kissing and embracing each other on the dance floor that night. The inconsequential details of the moment were not what mattered though; the dissolution of his presence from my life became an evident option as neither of us promised any obligation or commitment to stay in our courtship. Since I never compromised myself for this relationship, my dignity remained intact. I was in a trance for maybe a day, mostly because I couldn't believe my own ability to decipher truth so quickly, but also because I realized the purpose of our interaction.

Somehow, I thought I was flawed. I listened to so many people in my past say things like, "You don't know it all," or "Your expectations are unrealistically high," or "Nothing I do is ever good enough," that I started to distrust my own ability to sense accurately when a relationship no longer served my purpose. I stayed in what seemed like endless battles, because I started to believe that in order to have real love, you have to fight for it. I also started to believe that love takes time, and there are some hardships that you will have to bear, but that's what makes your love-ship even stronger, to endure the hard times. I no longer trusted myself to let go. Was I scared I would make the wrong decision and miss out on the love of my life?

I had made a conscious decision to dwell in ignorance and ignore my gift of intuition. I did not try to persuade the fabric of life by visualizing that I would be with this other person indefinitely. I simply asked, before meditation, through subtle intention, "Is this the relationship I am supposed to be in?"

The greater being, that which I am a part of, looks out for my best interest and clearly gives instructions on how to proceed with circumstances life lays before my feet.

What I know, is that this ignorance is one of the main reasons we have discourse in our intimate relationships, and why various multitudes of relationships fail to continue or strengthen in healthy ways. How many of us pay no mind to our gifts or choose to ignore our innate intuition in the presence of perceived happiness? To tell the utmost truth, I had interest in this man for a long-term relationship, but chose not to enter into one out of pure love. Love for him and the new-found love I carried for myself. I wanted the best for the both of us.

There were many things about him that mirrored myself. He even expressed, "I can be myself," and, "I feel like we are the same," during our conversations. This space I create for others to be vulnerable is a higher level of transparency I have achieved in spiritual practice. To become so transparent and open, that when a person looks at you, they can only see a reflection of themselves. This is the God within me operating in perfect harmony. We are the same, silly boy. Looking at

38

others is the real-deal mirror work. Instead of staring at a reflection of yourself, stare at the actions of others and you will notice what you like about yourself shows up in them as well as what you don't like. The dislikes that appear in others should allow us to treat each other more humanely, and increase our capacity for compassion. Therefore, I was hurt when he told me he thought he loved someone else, but there were no hard feelings and I hoped we could be good friends in the future.

At the end of our season, I opened my heart and decided to tell this man that I loved him enough to release him. In truth I did and always will, but from a distance. You see, in order to be present in your space, others must adhere to the experience of your boundaries. Go ahead, sound like your parents and say it! "If you want to live under the roof of this house, you must abide by my rules." Your body is your temple, your peace of mind. Your surroundings, the milieu is your house, and if another wants to live there with you, what are your rules?

The only thing we can do as a loving action is to let people go. To hold on, to force, to coerce is just another method to control and manipulate people for your own comfort. Do not attempt to try to prevent events from occurring; you cannot stop someone from doing what they want to do. What matters is not our tactics of prevention or even the actual event that occurs. People who have mastered emotional intelligence dwell in the consistency and resiliency in how they respond to a situation. If you are cursed by your worst enemy, are you more likely to curse them back or to turn and walk away? When someone does something in your life that goes against your morals, do you look to find the purpose in the lesson, or do you cry out asking the universe, why me? You may have failed multiple times at getting to a particular goal, but the best part is that even though you have tripped, you have the power to get back up, even closer to the goal than before when you started. Look to see in which direction you fell. Because even if you trip, stumble, and fall over the finish line, you still have won the race. Failure is what propels so many people into greatness. Only from this place can you learn thousands of ways not to get where you're trying to go.

When you learn yourself, never dim your light, your spirit, your personality, your God Spark.

Suppression of our gifts is always from a place of fear. We feel like if we are our most authentic selves, then certain individuals won't want us to be a part of their lives. Hiding the truest version of ourselves so we don't stand out amongst the crowd is a safe haven, and we have come to believe that things will stay consistent and safe if we don't step too far out the box. But how could this be, when life is in an everlasting, ever-reacting, ever-experiencing rate of manifestation? Why do we expect to remain idle within a mass of energy that is constantly moving and changing? Even when we believe our physical bodies are sitting still, we are still moving and changing constantly. Learning how to let go of what others may think of us and live freely in who we are is what can bring us freedom from the suppression of our energy. And when we don't suppress our very nature, that is when true living begins.

If others decide they don't want to be a part of your amazing life, then that is okay too. Don't deny yourself this simple truth, that everything that happens in life is only there to push you into a greater field of consciousness. To deny this truth is to deny the essence of who and what you are. You are trying to remove yourself from yourself for just a few people by not going after your dreams, sacrificing your wants and likes, and putting yourself last. But I finally figured out that with the billions of people in the world, there are thousands you can just be yourself around. You just have to go out and meet them. Do not continue to step down from your holy pedestal, remove your crown, walk amongst the vineyard, eating of the unripe fruit, and pulling the weeds from between your toes in peasant's clothing, and then wonder why no one recognizes who you are. If you feel you are a queen, it's okay to claim your royalty and dress the part. You don't have to camouflage your colors to blend in with your surroundings. You were made to stand out, to add color and texture. You were made to be exactly who you are.

You have a light that you bring when you step into a room. Have you somewhere, somehow dimmed your light? Did you put a dimmer on your light switch or pick up a bulb with less wattage along the way? Have you been in a relationship with a partner who told you your voice was too loud, and then found yourself being quiet even when he is not around? What is the cost when you suffocate the light of your spirit? Did you think God built you to blend in? This light will shine on all your stories and make it so others can connect to the perseverance in your journey. Too long you have compromised, converted, settled down, mutually agreed on, and for what? Do not continue ignoring your own needs. Trust yourself, and do not give up on your own dreams for the sake of your neighbor.

When you finally recognize your greatness, by embracing the characteristics that make you special, you begin to illuminate. You may want to laminate your greatness and wear it around your neck, put it in a customized frame, and hang it on your walls, but I am telling you there will be no need for this. People can sense your inner greatness far more easily than they can see the external evidence. You'll start to carry your uniqueness at your center and beams of pure light will shoot from your orifices and fingertips and the roof of your temple. But you must be prepared for what good the light shows inside of yourself and what ugliness it shows others about themselves.

You see, when your light shines brightly, it may reveal some unresolved issues and past hurts that other people covered up. Your light may shine so radiantly that you see people for who they really are and not what they have dressed themselves up to be. Some people around you, sometimes people you've known for your entire life-cycle, will become angry at you because your light exposes the secrets they didn't even know they had. Even if the only change that occurs is in how you treat yourself, and how you love yourself, some people will become defensive because they realize, by watching your self-love, how much they haven't loved themselves. Some people will say that you've changed, and in truth, when your spirit vibrates at a level of higher frequency, full of self-acceptance, it fully activates within the time-space continuum. Since we are all connected, others can pick up on the vibration of that frequency. They may become bothered by the way you view yourself, and their fear of not measuring up can be projected onto you. They fear that you may forget about them, because you finally remembered yourself. Sometimes remembering who we are, causes us to reevaluate the company we keep. Sometimes, because they remain lost, they are uncomfortable to be in the presence of one who is all-knowing and all-being.

People may become irritated by what you say, why you do, and where you are, because they agree fundamentally with what you say you are.

However, in their agreement they can't help but to see how they have dimmed their own light and then start to feel threatened because you reactivated yours. They will shut themselves away because of their own feelings of lack and inadequacy. I like to refer to this as the spirit deficit.

It is easy to detect those who have a spirit deficit. When in contact with these people, you will start to feel drained, as if the energy is being sucked right out of you. They draw on your energy to fill themselves up and make themselves temporarily feel good. They do not believe, accept, or realize the importance of self-actualization. These non-believers will become discouraged by not being able to live up to your unspoken expectations. Near the fire that burns inside of you, they feel scorched and that their own spark may never compare. Another one of the greatest universal truths that they have yet to realize is that they are enough.

Always remember, you were born enough. What is for you, is for you. Your blessings had your name on them before you were even of this world, as well as others. And finally, when you find yourself, in yourself, amongst yourself, become unmovable in that knowing. Be still, as the force you know you are, for no one can move you from the realm in which you truly come from.

HEAL YOURSELF INTENTIONALLY

Your Deepest Pain Is the Birthplace of Your Greatest Creation

One of the greatest things about being hurt, left, and not chosen, is that you have been hurt, left, and not chosen. Many of the greatest people who grace the pages of our history books have survived the toughest of times. When you learn how to use pain to your advantage, it can yield some of the most immeasurable results. Life only affords you tenacity, faith, and unwavering courage when you experience some of your lowest points and make it through to the other side. When you hit rock bottom, and there is nothing to surround you but darkness, you only have one option. Use your imagination! Imagination just happens to be the stuff that dreams are made of, the place where cures for cancer are found, and the playground in which master builders go to reconstruct their lives.

If you intend it, it will come.

Living intentionally may be one of the simplest and hardest things you've ever had to do. To do each thing in your life with reason, requires you to exert control over your primal urges and your other five senses. Creating the roadmap to your destiny is a soul contract between your heart, your mind, and your spirit. We tend to be our harshest critics because we are the first ones notified when we break our own rules. So, do yourself a favor through this journey. Be easy with yourself.

When I first entered into a contract with myself, I didn't realize that part of learning how to love myself was learning how to trust myself. Or that trusting myself meant keeping my own word to me. The most important person you will ever keep your word to is yourself. I externalized my own inability to keep up with goals, my own procrastination, my own lack of following a diet or exercise regime onto other people. When those attributes came up in others, they made me furious. One of my biggest pet peeves was the inability of others to keep their word, but I was only super-vigilant and supersensitive of what others were doing in every little situation, because a part of that thing that drove me furious actually existed within me.

The problem is not that we don't trust other people, the problem is that we don't trust ourselves. I used to be one of those people who went into the grocery store without a list, and then left the store having spent more than I intended to spend. I used to go to the drive-thru at a fast food restaurant with the intention of getting a small number eight combo with a bottled water, and instead opted for the promotional rainbow shake delight, because the flash advertisement yelled, "2 for $5!" Or even better, if the worker at the drive-thru window asked me to upgrade my meal at no cost, or because it was cheaper, that was like hitting the jackpot. I mean, who isn't happy to get a good deal? However, if the object was not what you intended to buy, if it is not what you intended to eat, and if it is not the deal you intentionally went out for, chances are it is NOT a GOOD deal! So, what is your response when you can get more food for less money than what you originally came for? If that makes you happy then don't be surprised if you also get more weight than what you came for.

When every clear intention is outweighed by an external force, you sabotage yourself and a price will be paid. Ask yourself, are you willing to continue paying the price? Are you willing to continue living an undesirable life that you no longer wish to call your own? Or, are you willing to make the necessary changes to live at your maximum capacity? Intention is a guide, a principle, a character trait of integrity.

Do what you say you're going to do, and if you're not going to do it, don't say it at all.

The art of intention holds immeasurable benefits in transforming every area of your life, not just those centered around superficial things like the food we eat or the clothes we wear. Do you intend to live the life of your dreams, or don't you? It really is as simple as that. Go into the world being the type of person you intend to be. Be the type of person you wish to attract, someone you are proud to be around. Get comfortable and excited about dropping your own name. Be intentionally loving to yourself and your biggest cheerleader.

When you start changing your spiritual direction, it's going to take time and patience. The journey to get there will be ongoing, and for some it may take a little longer than others, but you have a minute-by-minute choice to live your personal best version of your life. The most important step, that is often looked over, is first knowing exactly what it is you want out of your life. When you have no idea of how you'd like your life to run, what career you'd enjoy the most, what you'd like your health to look like, it is easy to slip in with the accordance of how others want your life to be. Someone else's ideas, a la carte will slide onto your plate, either through inheritance, social norms, or something you just happened to hear along the way that became simply, "the right thing to do." And now you sit in front of a pile of Brussel sprouts, wondering how they ever appeared on your plate. How can you attract authentic relationships and life experiences if you have no idea of what your own authenticity means? Who are you and what do you want? How are you to love anyone else, if your actions contradict loving yourself? How are others to trust you, when you cannot trust yourself?

When a new person comes into my life who likes to go out and hang in the bar all the time, that is not someone I want present in my space on a consistent basis. If someone whom I call my friend, gets so drunk they have to sleep in their car, or they exhibit reckless behavior such as indulging in sexual experiences without knowing the other person's STD status; if that person says things like, "I just enjoy life as it comes," and they have no plan, I run! These people have no value for their own lives, so how can they have value for mine? You should not expect someone to love you who has not yet learned how to love themselves. I cannot place my being in the midst of happenstance and hope for the best. If I decide to go along with whatever life brings, then I should not be angry when the world and people come at me with their own agendas. This is not to say, that any of the behavior I've described above is good or bad. No one is better or worse than anyone else. This is only to say, know your spirit intimately, and the experiences that you intentionally want to have.

I cannot trust you when you say you love me, if you clearly exhibit behaviors that contradict you loving yourself.

Hear me when I say this: talk is cheap! In matters of the heart, look into the meaning of other's actions and not into the meaning of their words. If you do not invest in intention in your own life, and instead let intoxicants or stimulants guide your decision making; if you make a comment that's passive-aggressive, and within the same breath follow up that sentence with, "Just playing," I take my life very seriously, and I don't play like that. It should not be your intention, nor is it required of you to teach another what you know, especially if that person is either unwilling or unready to learn. Your acceptance of not being able to teach everyone, everything, or to become someone that everyone likes is something you must grow to be okay with. Each person's life is truly their own, and the only one you are entirely responsible for throughout your life, is the one God breathed into your own body. It is you! What I've learned and what I know, is that great things come to those who bait. And intention in your life is like the bait to your dreams, so cast your net wide and let's begin.

Download Your Free Intentional Living Checklist at

www.breakingbravely.com

When your intentions align your life for its greater purpose, the universe will send the resources required. The source will speak to you so loudly, so clearly, and so perfectly, if only you will be still enough, long enough, and willing enough to listen. Just imagine all the things you'd be capable of if you became willing to accept the task that is given. Within my personal journey, I still to this day ask for what I'd like to attract. But I also follow up my request by asking whether what I want to attract is best for the greater good. If a million dollars offers me no transcendence to a higher level of consciousness, then where is the value in that million dollars? I ask, and then listen to every little sign life affords me.

I remember daydreaming about a lavender dress that I would wear during the upcoming summer and a very particular hue of nail polish that I thought would complement it beautifully. I often visualize with as much detail as possible, since the mind cannot tell the difference between a perceived visualization and an actual representation of the wanted outcome. After getting my hair done the very next day, when I was paying at the register, I looked to the right and saw "my nail polish!" I was already in a feeling space of happiness and gratitude, and then life showed up. That day, I did not purchase the nail polish because that was not my intention when I went into the store, but I did thank the universe for its constant reminders; the reminders and universal truths that I am loved, I am safe, I am guided, I can have whatever my heart desires, and that I am a part of the great I, AM.

Committing to a daily spiritual practice became just as routine as my morning coffee. I heard from many spiritual gurus of the need to create space for a time of spiritual awareness daily as they did, but often gave myself excuses and thought my mentors were super heroes. By making them super heroes, it meant we were not the same, and gave me an excuse to be less than they were. Therefore, I didn't have to hold myself accountable, because we were not held to the same standard, until I intentionally made sure we were, until I made the choice to live as the woman I wanted to become, and not as the woman I had known myself to be.

Once you establish a spiritual routine, the most significant change begins to stir your soul. I could feel the rhythm of life during meditation, swaddling me, and at the same time unwrapping me like a child's Christmas gift. I started unraveling so fast, that the quiet spun me into a whole different dimension. I ended up on the path to my true identity. Are you ready to find your path?

Get Ready to Make Room

On one particular Michigan rainy/snowy/slushy morning, when it had been 60 degrees and sunny the previous day, I prayed for a couple of things in my life, and then sat in meditation. I had to wake up at 4:45 am, to be on the treadmill for twenty minutes, perform my "I am" affirmations, complete my gratitude journaling, and write in my book, while taking a bath, so I could be done by 6 am. Then I was off to get the first of my kids up by 6:15 and away to school by 6:50, the second by 8:00, and the third by 8:30, and lastly myself to work. Amongst the things that I asked for that morning to bring me more joy, were more friends and more love.

I had an ex-boyfriend, and at that time I had not yet found the absolute need to release his presence from my life, until that very day. One thing was consistent in our relationship towards the end; the only thing he ever did was make me cry. I had hoped to be friends, but came to the realization that we could not be friends in that space and time.

On this particular day, I performed my spiritual routine just like any other day. I ate healthy foods, but by mid-day I was literally exhausted. My ex-boyfriend and I had a conversation earlier in the week via text message and the conversation still bothered me. During that day, I realized that our talk had settled into my spirit like a plague and that I was being unintentional with the things that were most important, like my boundaries, my space, my time, and what and whose energy I subjected myself to. I realized his presence in my life was toxic. I had to become intentional about the people I subjected myself to, otherwise it could throw off other areas that I was intentional in or felt good about. Toxic people are not toxic because they are bad people. Toxic people are toxic because they distract you from your purpose.

This one text conversation, from earlier in the week had sent the rest of my week into a tizzy. I was mentally exhausted from our conversation. The thoughts of what things could mean and how they could be perceived ran through my mind like a teenage love story. I had not been diligent in protecting myself from what I could absorb by speaking with the wrong person. Protect yourself from what you listen to, what you watch, what you taste, what you inhale, and what you touch. Your soul is sacred and impenetrable, but through the five senses your mind and your heart are impressionable.

This one dialogue with my ex gave me dreams at night and nightmares during the day. It disturbed my being so much, I began to cry in the middle of my work day, trying to function. It distracted me from my greatness, dulled my beauty, and so I asked the source, if it was this one being, that caused such distress? If so, I agreed to leave this person alone, and then blocked him on my phone.

Within the next couple of hours after blocking this person, some amazing things happened. I had so much love pouring out of my heart, it became hard to contain. I had one of the best supportive and wisdom-filled conversations with an old friend of mine that called out of the blue. It was unbelievable. I even set up a time when I would visit her and see her new baby girl. I then got on the phone and asked another long-term friend who had moved out of state, how far she lived from me, because I wanted to go visit her during the summer. She replied that she was already coming to Michigan in July, missed me, and was going to ask if she could come and see me! Another couple of friends through social media reached out to me shortly thereafter, and made plans for us to get together for the upcoming weekend. Suddenly my life and my heart were booked solid with loads of love and friends.

In this moment I knew, because I simply believe that nothing happens by coincidence, that I made space intentionally to receive all that I had asked for. Once the energy that promoted disruption in my life was removed, this space created room for all new energy to flow through. So, I opened up all the doors and windows of my soul and let the love flow in. This doesn't mean that I stopped loving my ex, or that I ever will, but it did mean I love my peace and intentionality enough to protect it at all costs. After all, when a gallon of milk spoils and starts to stink, you don't sit in the middle of the kitchen floor rocking it back and forth thinking about all the good bowls of cereal you've shared. You make a decision to pour that garbage down the drain and go purchase a new gallon. Make decisions for everything in your life the same way, and make room for all the friends, all the love, and all the abundance you could ever ask for.

Let your "No" stand for something, even against the little things.

I had to learn to even say no to the littlest of things, and sometimes this came into effect with my children. If a task was not a part of my daily to-do list, either I would intentionally add it to a near date in the future, or I would decide not to do the task at all. But learning not to back down or back out was a process. I began to rationalize why being intentional was too extreme. "But it's only a five-dollar pizza," I would tell myself. Or, when the kids would ask if we could go see a movie, since they had been sitting in the house all day, I would tell myself, "But it's only a movie." However, I did not allow my justifications to give me a pass to do whatever came to my mind and especially whatever came to their minds. I mean, really. Who was the parent here?

Now this doesn't mean that they never received what they asked for. This only means that there were no more "spur of the moment" decisions. I wanted to teach my children that it was okay to be bored! Life is not always a rollercoaster waiting around the corner every five-seconds. You have to be intentional in being still and creating peace. I also didn't want to teach them that I would go back on my word or that my time didn't matter. Doing this would only have turned them into women who felt their time didn't matter.

If I planned to cook dinner at home, I stuck to my plans. It is always best to have some sort of plan for your day. The pizza and movie moved into my next day's intention. I went hard at this plan and was determined to see how intention would set my life apart from the one I owned for so many years before. If it was my goal to write a book, I had to determine what that looked like. I set the intention not to go to bed late so I could get up early, not to make up excuses or spend 45 minutes scrolling through social media. I made up my mind not to let activities come and blindside me with things I considered more fun to do. Until there was at least one action taken within the plan of my day, I shifted my mind from one of many things to do to just doing one non-negotiable. This plan is the way to get things accomplished. It was up to me to be the change, so I was, and life hasn't since steered me wrong.

We need to start our days with more non-negotiables.

RADICAL FORGIVENESS

I Never Knew My Capacity to Love, Until I Cried for the Person Who Hurt Me the Most

For me, forgiving all the people who I thought hurt me was not only a lifeline, but a sister to my gratitude. I always heard people speak of gratitude as if it were a key to the door where the life of my dreams waited for me on the other side. I kept a daily gratitude journal, but was primarily grateful for all the "good" things I attracted into my life. I don't think the majority of people spend most of their prayers of gratitude on what they consider "painful events." We tend to be partial towards ceremonies and traditions; the graduations, weddings, baby showers, and holidays. These are the times when people are most grateful. Within our seasons of gift-showering is where we physically show up. But where we spiritually show up is in times of turmoil and despair. Those are the times in which you can really see how far people have come and the growth within.

Most people would be thrilled to win a million dollars. It doesn't take much effort to try to get a lottery winner to be happy with the fact that they will receive enough wealth to make all of their financial dreams come true. But just imagine how hard it is to convince people of the blessings they receive while in their greatest pain; that in their darkest hour, they stand at the doorstep to their greatest creation.

People don't usually stand in line, thanking God for a loved one dying of a terminal illness. When a special relationship, one that we placed all our dreams in fails, we normally take it out on the other person. This blame takes up so much room in our hearts that it stunts our growth. The blame also either diminishes or entirely takes away our expectations. Out of fear we build a wall so we can never be hurt again. We want to be thankful, but only for what we want to be thankful for. This reason is why forgiveness is so important. The universe is waiting. All you have to do is make room. And the very first place you should choose to make room is in your heart.

I had to let go of some things to make room for your love; one of them was my ego.

Back at the spiritual classroom where God is seated, forgiveness gets a hall pass when the room begins acting out. Forgiveness and abandonment don't even live on the same block. They go to the same school, but are specialties under a different curriculum. In order for you to transform any area of your life with success, you must learn to move away from your old neighborhood of habits and old ways of thinking. You must start to surround yourself with a new crowd. The people you seek should be spiritual elders who can give you a quantum leap in your wisdom and ability to create the life you deserve. You can spot a spiritual elder by their capacity to forgive, and in their ability to be an observer of an event without taking things personally. How do you become friends with your enemies? Master the art of not taking anything personally.

Your mercy provides a shift that you may not have given as much attention as needed before. This shift allows you to move beyond yourself and experience empathy. Forgiveness does not make you powerless, it makes you powerful. It brightens the dark corners that negative energy once filled. It opens your lungs for life to flow through you, like a breath of fresh air. Mercy gives you the wings to fly amidst a barren sky, in which you may see a neighboring bird only every five to ten miles. There is room in forgiveness because it is difficult, and the majority of people gravitate towards what is simple and easy. It is easy to hold a grudge. It is easy to ignore another soul. And it is even easier to forget those that caused you hurt as if they never even existed. But where is the glory in that? You are the creator of all things present and not present in your life. You make the choice of what you wish to let go and what you wish to carry on. And if you choose to carry a wrongdoing done to you, you are the only one that its weight will tear down.

One day long ago, I simply chose not to carry anything for anyone else anymore. I forgave everyone for everything, and I realized the burden we carry to live out our dreams is often heavy enough all on its own. Each person owes themselves the responsibility of birthing the unique gift God placed inside of them. And we should not expect to give off or receive any burden other than the one we inherit. We are our own answer, our own desire, our own breakdown, and at the same time our own breakthrough. And so, I even forgave the people I hadn't met yet for things that hadn't been done. And finally, I forgave myself for considering that any battle of anyone else's was my fight to be won. When people tried to gift me with their boxes packed with shame, blame, and guilt, forgiveness cured my curiosity to see what was in the box, and helped me to write in big bold letters, "RETURN TO SENDER."

We drag debilitating stories beside us like security blankets we carry as a demanding infant. I often envisioned all the hurt I held onto as the bags I carried for my elderly mother while shopping. At first, she would want me to hold her purse because it was heavy, and she couldn't quite maneuver her cane like she wanted to. And then even though I told her it was 85 degrees outside, she all of a sudden got hot and wants me to hold her winter coat. Instead of leaving her purse in the car, she requested to bring it because there just might be something that she needs inside. And a lighter jacket isn't even considered a possibility because, "You never know what Michigan weather is going to be."

At this point I am now considered to be her personal motorized shopping cart, complete with GPS navigation. I often become a companion with stories to tell and keep her content. And the shopping trip gets to the point where I am carrying a load so heavy, including shopping bags and the leftovers from the restaurant, that I think, "Maybe she's going to slip me a twenty," because obviously I've changed careers and have become her personal bellhop. But no, she makes me feel bad for not wanting to carry all of these things. Things that she didn't even need in the first place, but she made herself believe she couldn't be without them. And now, I can't be without them.

We find ourselves offering to carry more and more bags for other people. You start stuffing bags within bags to make more room in your hands for the handles. You shift the bags from one hand to the other to relieve some of the discomfort of the red, hot, indentations that have started to appear on your palms. When waiting in long lines, half of your body shifts to the right to compensate for all the extra weight you've accumulated on the left. And then you stand on one foot at the checkout lane and tell yourself it's a good thing, because this position is like a Standing Tree pose. You're not broken down, you're doing yoga! You're burning calories and building a rock-solid core at the same time, right? This is awesomeness! Isn't it funny?! We come up with all sorts of ways to justify why it's okay to allow ourselves to be uncomfortable. How then, does the discomfort become as natural as the air we breathe, to the point where we take ourselves for granted?

When you think of things that people may have done to you, whether you believe it was out of spite or out of ignorance, I want you to visualize turning those things into labels and then putting those labels onto bags. I want you to visualize brown paper bags with handles. I want you to pretend like each unforgiven thing is a product that you have picked up along your travels throughout life. Not only do I want you to place the things you know are unforgiven in a bag, I want you to create a bag for each unknown thing you haven't forgiven. I know what you're thinking, "How can I forgive someone for something, if I don't even know what it is?" The truth is, you do know what it is; you just haven't asked yourself. So go ahead, ask yourself, and let whatever comes out your mouth become a possibility, because it is a possibility. In order for something to come out of your mouth it has to have been created and already exist. No matter how crude, ugly, or against your morality these things that come out your mouth or into your thinking may be, I want you to listen. This exercise will definitely be a testament in facing your own inner demons. I want you to get as real with yourself as possible.

I then want you to visualize the person you are forgiving. For some of you this will mean turning to yourself. Who is it exactly, that handed you that particular bag? I want you to repeat to that person or to the mirror, "I'm begging your pardon. Please, forgive me, but these bags are not my own." You say the previous phrase to yourself, to the visual of the person's face you are holding in your mind's eye, and then you say it out loud.

I knew in the beginning of this journey you prepared to bring some things along that wouldn't be necessary, and I bit my tongue, and let you bring them anyway. On top of the fact that you are not physically or spiritually able to carry your own burdens, you have laid them at my feet, draped them across my shoulders and flung them on my back, as if I had nothing going on before you came along. Like I was sitting dormant within my being, waiting for you to tell me in which direction to go. Well, I'm sorry for bursting your bubble, but when I am carrying your bags, I am simply unable to carry my own. So let me tell you, what we are not going to do.

I am not going to continue running back to the car to put things in the trunk because then I cannot enjoy my time or my day with you as I planned. And trunk space can sometimes become storage space, a space people put things they are not ready to let go of. I need my trunk space! You must not know how much I enjoy shoe shopping, or mountain biking, book writing, or cooking, or whatever else I might need my trunk space for. I don't feel guilty, I've paid for my space and now it's time that you get your own. Two trunks are better than one.

I cannot go all the places I would like to go, simply because the burden of both of our loads is simply too much for only one person to carry. This love-ship requires teamwork. And if you want to continue to be in love, you have to work with me. I forgive you for not realizing how this might make me feel. I forgive you for not responding to my feelings in a loving way, and I forgive me for allowing myself to pick up your things in the first place. Unfortunately, this is where the pony ride stops, with love and with forgiveness.

Now, I am by no means giving people permission to stop carrying their parents' groceries into the house. I do not want a full email box from angry mommies and daddies blaming me for their children no longer taking them to bingo or to the casino. However, forgiveness is still necessary between parents and children. For things said and things unsaid; for things done and things undone.

Forgiveness is letting go of every other possibility other than the truth that occurred. It is to be free of blame, for yourself and for others. Forgiveness is being open to other possibilities when you find yourself becoming the CSI investigator on "why" people act a certain way. It is acceptance of the reason they gave you, if you were lucky enough to get one, and all the reasons that they didn't give you. Forgiveness is the knowing that you will be okay. Whatever the reason is for why people do what they do, that reason has absolutely nothing to do with you. Most people don't even know for themselves why they do the things they do. Sometimes it's out of habit, and at other times the brain is on cruise control, to do what it has been conditioned to do. For those who feel they do not owe you an explanation, or they do not want to say anything that will let you down, forgive their silence, because maybe they simply have not mastered the ability to communicate the way they feel in any other way. A heart set to love on auto-pilot does not necessarily let them off the hook, but it does provide you with the clarity that some things that cannot be explained.

Forgive people for the truth in the event that occurred; it is not so much important what happened, but how you respond to it. Every event is the result of two or more people.

Recently I initiated a deeper relationship with a childhood friend. We grew up together, and at this one point in our lives, I was hoping to become more present, increasing the frequency of our conversation and the quality of our bonding experience. When we were together, the moments were full of excitement and calmness, restoration and healing. It was a safe place that allowed us to fully express who we were without the conditioning of external commonalities.

One day, I reached out to my friend on the telephone and there was no answer when I called. Not only was there no answer, but there was no call back, nor any contact for the next week. Initially I was hurt. I was hurt because I felt a loss, but with reflection I worked past my hurt and was able to reach out again in a loving way. My friend replied that he had been going through some depression, but was better at the time I called. I then thanked God for his present state of feeling, wished him the best, let him know I would be there if he ever needed me, and created space for him to be present with his own reality.

I chose not to make his experience about me. Yes, he was posting things on social media during our period of non-communication that "appeared" to be fun. One possibility was that he simply chose to move on with his life without so much as saying goodbye. But since I know depression, I also know that being out with people, purchasing things, and posting bright smiling pictures may not authentically represent a true inner balance and peace. These compensations do not represent true happiness at all. Social media is simply where you go to post your "best social self" the best version of yourself that you want people to see, when they don't "know" the real you. People may have no idea what you as a person are really going through. That same person, smiling and laughing on the outside, can be crying for help on the inside. Accept the other person's truth even if you cannot see it with your eyes or hear it with your ears, for it is their truth that God gave to them in that moment. You cannot convince someone of your truth, if they are invested in only seeing a situation one way. You must allow them to believe what they are ready to believe. Their ability to seek out new opportunities to push they're thinking and growth is only a reflection of their own personal journey, the one that we all are entitled to possess.

Where Manipulation Resides, Forgiveness is Always Required, Purpose is Always Present

When some people enter into your life, it is their intention to do you harm, but most people mean to do good. The harm that they cause is actually a favor to disrupt your soil, so that good seed may be planted on fertile ground. It is my belief that some people are put here to be reconstructors. A reconstructor's purpose is to tear down a person, situation, place, or thing, to push them into rebuilding. They go throughout life, tearing down and rebuilding, over and over again, reincarnating in the time-space continuum, manifested as flesh. However, you may be so hurt by the disruption of your comfort, you become too focused on the tearing down. And once we focus on what's being torn down, we can never make it past the empty construction site to enjoy the new city being built. We keep on trying to rebuild on the same spot instead of searching for new land. And most people ache so deeply for consistency, that when what they have always known becomes disrupted, they feel reality is distorted. Since their reality is distorted, they can no longer recognize who they are, because they solely associated themselves with only the areas of stagnation in their lives. However, life works the other way around. Reality is distorted in complacency, and the reality of your being calls for constant change and growth.

Reconstructors are some of the most intimately lonely people you'll ever meet. They have a hard time finding people who can take their level of constructive criticism. Reconstructors are often in careers such as transformational coaching, and teaching positions. To be in an intimate relationship with someone who rebuilds your life for your own well-being, takes a certain amount of finesse and extreme vulnerability. Sometimes we are okay with our partners transforming other's lives, as long as it is not our own. We, by no means want someone trying to tell us what to do. But reconstructors are feelers, God-sent, and a lot of the time they can view your life from the outside as a non-biased observer and tell you exactly what you need to do to create the life you deserve. A soft and gentle approach is not normally an enduring characteristic of reconstructors, because in order to transform people's lives, they have to possess the ability to reach inside that person's spirit and pull out the things they didn't want themselves or anyone else to see. Bulldozers are not gentle pieces of equipment, but they are some of the most effective at getting the job done.

Reconstructors in your life are also gladiators for your success and spiritual welfare. They will hear what no one else has heard and see what no one else has seen. Amongst them, people feel as comfortable as they ever have been in their lives. People will feel they can truly be themselves, and that they can connect on a different level than with anyone else. However, they will also tell you things about yourself, that other people are afraid of saying. Therefore, they can develop a love-hate relationship with those who cannot see their true intention. People tend to admire reconstructors for their strength and resiliency, but also find them harsh. They provide a consistent tough love, and unless you are ready for tough love, their bear claws will hurt.

Reality is distorted in complacency; the reality of your being calls for constant change and growth.

Disconnect happens because most people in intimate relationships are looking for someone to make them feel better about themselves. People are generally not looking to grow, because with growth comes growing pains. By all means, the mind protects us against discomfort and perceived loss of life. To be close with a reconstructor and to be intimate is a balance that is rare, but is also among the most holy and sought after. In the ultimate experience of intimate relationships, two people in each other's presence, reach into each other and bring out so much good, they both change the world. They both are so whole there is no shadow amidst the light. There is no place to hide, nor is there anything to hide, they can be the truest version of themselves at all times.

Forgive People for Not Seeking Past What They Were Taught

Sometimes people may not have had the proper caregivers in their young childhood years to give them tools to show them what it meant to love themselves or to love others. So, as an adult, they act out of dysfunction. They become thieves, taking what they want and need from you, and deceiving you to get it. A lot of times these people don't even have a choice in making these decisions; they are ignorant of their actions. The inner child is only ego, and operates unaffected by the hurt it causes those around it. Every person comes into your life to give and to take. We are all giving and taking something at some level from one another. What you have to continuously decipher is how much of yourself, you are willing to give away.

For instance, would you forgive the rapist of an elderly person sooner than you would forgive the rapist of a child? In both situations, the intent was to gain control and even love, to a certain extent, so what difference is there in the age at which the person is raped? Is it because the physical body is within different developmental stages? If the child is too young to remember or the elderly person has Alzheimer's, does this weigh in on our sentencing? If it was the mother or child of the antichrist, even though we are taught to love, is then the crime permissible? How many of you clap and rejoice in the death of world terrorists, because it is our troops against theirs? I tell you this, for every life a purpose exists, different and the same as your own, and to rejoice in murder, regardless of the offense, makes us hypocritical. You cannot be for murder and against murder at the same time, or can you?

Under certain circumstances, we bend the law of life and death, especially when it comes to protecting ourselves from a perceived threat. Should we not be forgiven for what we feel we have to do? At a certain level, people who hurt us are only living out experiences, acting out on people, and reaching out for things externally, because they are protecting themselves and doing what they feel they must. I personally, don't have to wonder why a person did a certain thing, to show empathy and compassion. I do not agree to be a part in every circumstance, but just because I didn't contribute does not mean I lack the ability to understand. Since we are all connected, to separate from or not see the depth of another is only to deny a part of yourself. Therefore, I am my brother's keeper, and every being is my brother or sister.

If that being boasts that they did the horrible thing on purpose, that the event brought them pleasure or gave them life, that deed was still rooted in purpose. For without the presence of what we consider horrible things we would not be able to enjoy all the beautiful things. Be careful not to base your perception of their boasting off of the way you see or hear them. The way you feel about them can be as inaccurate or accurate as a Western Blot test. It is all based on what you choose to believe.

We are preconditioned to believe in numbers and percentages to give us a certain level of predictability. The scientific community has statistics for every minute thing on the face of the planet, but some things cannot be explained. The exception to what we learned exists way more often than we allow ourselves to imagine. As a matter a fact, if we permitted ourselves to imagine more than to hold steadfast to concrete beliefs we have been taught, the percentages for rates of disease would decrease. Out of fear, we associate free thinking with chaos. Our society is governed by a set of rules. You must obey the law of the land, and I believe most people do obey the law, yet, chaos still exists.

If it was your child, that did a hideous thing, would you forgive them? Forgive others with the same amount of love as you would forgive your children, even if they meant you harm or are proud of causing you pain. The best thing is that if you survived your darkest times, now you have a choice never to let it happen again and to avoid similar hurt in the future. If you don't forgive however, you will receive the lesson over and over again. Look for the lesson and then receive the gift.

Forgive the Residual of Each Event

The Residual, as I like to call it, is all the things that have become associated with one given event. The residual of the event includes all the parts that are unforgiven that you and the other person aren't even aware of. For example, if someone is adopted into a loving, caring family, this does not mean they will perceive it this way. Not only may they need to forgive the feelings of abandonment from childhood, but if the environment wasn't nurturing and the child got abused, they may then blame the biological parent for something that was not a direct result of the parent's decision, but a residual event related to the circumstances.

The more things you declare out loud that you forgive the person for, the more you may surprise yourself. When my ex-fiancé finally moved on, I started to speak out loud the current event of forgiveness and the residual. It was similar to this:

I forgive you for leaving me. I forgive you for making me a single mother again. I forgive you for not having an answer for the children when they ask where you are. I forgive you for moving on, even though I am the one who told you to go. I forgive you for not begging to have me back or not putting in as much effort as I thought the girls or I deserved.

I have met with people from all walks of life that had to forgive a multitude of things. The offense is what keeps us stuck, while the other person continues to move forward with their lives. Forgive yourself and your perception that stood in your way to becoming free and letting go. Don't just stop at the lies, don't just stop at the cheating, the abuse, the sexual molestation; forgive people known and unknown for the residual. Your residual is the baggage you accumulated along the way, because to carry the bags was easier than letting go. You became a hoarder, a negativity magnet for dysfunction and set back. Now it's time to take a step back and break through!

The following are some examples of break-throughs my one-on-one coaching clients have journaled through radical forgiveness, and forgiveness of the residual.

Kelly's Journal of Forgiveness

A single mother with her bachelor's degree in nursing. She came home one day to find that the man she spent the last 16 years of her life with moved all of her personal belongings into a storage unit.

I forgive you for telling me to get my things and get out of your house. I forgive you for not caring or not knowing if I had anywhere else to go. I forgive you for making me homeless with our infant daughter. I forgive you for neglecting my trust, not recognizing my value, and for treating my spirit as anything less than the holy thing it is, has always been, and always will be. I forgive you for not calling when you said you were going to call. I forgive myself for putting up with unacceptable behavior.

I forgive my father for touching me. I forgive him for not showing me any other touch than intimate gestures that represented love from a man. I forgive everyone else in the world, because out of all the billions of people, not a single one heard me cry and came running through that door, of that small, dark, musty room to save me. I cried so loud, but no one heard me. No one except me, my father and God.

Make your forgiveness just as out-of-the-box as your gratitude. Speak and write your forgiveness into the universe as if it already exists. For those of you who would love support in how to exercise radical forgiveness, I have created the Breaking Bravely Forgiveness Journal. You can get your journal with an exclusive message from me at www.breakingbravely.com/forgivenessjournal

Keeping a forgiveness journal in which you forgive yourself and others in so many different, unconventional ways gives you permission to say all those things that have eaten away at you inside. Go ahead and say those things that you've always wanted to say, but didn't out of fear of retaliation or because you thought they would make you a "bad person." I felt such a release myself as I journaled while reading the forgiveness section of this book. I let things come out of my mouth that I didn't even necessarily believe were the root causes of the problem. But, if thoughts exist, then those thoughts are a part of the problem, and I couldn't afford to let one thing slide.

When you get to the point where you are in tears, that is where the work is. That is also where the hurt it, but where the hurt is the heart is, and healing is not too far behind. To write these thoughts, feelings, and hurts in your forgiveness journal, is just another form of creation, enhancing your ability to create and release. All your cards have to be laid out on the table, and you need to be completely honest with yourself. Forgive yourself for the things you know and the things you didn't know, then extend that kindness and courtesy to those in the world around you.

You can start your journal entries with the initial truth of each event, "What I forgive myself or that person most for, is _____. I forgive you for the hurt it caused. It caused me hurt because I felt a loss. I forgive you for my loss." And then forgive out loud what you blame the other person for! Everything you associated with that loss and all of it's residuals.

When people say, forgiveness is not for the other person, and it is more about yourself, this is true and untrue. Forgiveness is for everyone involved. The grudge that you may have held onto for the past 10 years? Most of the time, the other person involved doesn't even remember what happened. If they do, that has not stopped them from moving on. Don't sit and rue the fact that it is now forgotten, and rest in disbelief, telling yourself, "If it was that important to you, why hasn't it affected you like it affected me?" This is only wishing negative feelings into the lives of others to make yourself feel better. Would you really feel better, if your ex died from the heartache of leaving you? I ask you then, where is the integrity in that? Do you require that much of an apology? What if they have asked for forgiveness from God, is your forgiveness ranked higher than the Creator's? Someone else's discomfort, failure, or hurt should not produce winning feelings for you, for if one person loses we all lose.

John's Forgiveness Journaling to His Deceased Wife

When you left and went to heaven, I was angry. I was angry because I was not ready for you to go. I was angry because I had lost someone I love. In our vows, it said unto death do us part, but I always imagined we would have more time. That death did not come for the young, living their lives as philanthropists, volunteering abroad, with children at home who depend on them. In my head and my heart, death came to those that were prepared, were old, fragile, and weak. Death came for those who did bad things in the world or who had fulfilled their purpose. But you were not done, at least for my sake you weren't.

I forgive you for leaving me. I forgive you for not listening to the doctors or myself while you were here. I forgive you for not taking care of your health. I forgive you for living recklessly and leaving me behind. I forgive you for giving up and signing on for hospice services. I forgive you for leaving me all alone. I forgive you for the uncertainness I feel and the uncomfortableness that comes along with attempting to meet new romantic partners.

I forgive you for taking from me the thing I valued the most, being a husband, but most of all, modeling what a father and man should be to the mother of our beautiful children. I forgive you for not allowing them to see me at my fullest potential. I forgive you for the debility this has caused me at work and in how I function for the kids. I forgive you for my parents having to move in and help out. I forgive your scent on the pillow beside mine and the empty space on your side of the bed. I forgive your clothes for brushing my wrist when I walk into our closet. I forgive your laugh that plays in my memories and your hair for clogging up the sink.

I forgive you for thinking I didn't love you the same as before we were married. I forgive you for thinking all the insignificant things like stretch marks, cellulite, or chipped nail polish ever mattered. I forgive myself for not loving you enough to make you feel more secure. I forgive myself for not taking out the trash right when you asked me to. For not showing up on time for date night; all you wanted was for me to be on time. I forgive myself for not holding myself to a higher standard. You deserved that, and now that time can never be revisited. I forgive myself for not simply saying I'm sorry, and making you and our life the most important thing. It was the most important thing. It remains the most important thing.

I forgive everyone for their sympathy. Their intentions were good, but I do not require their sympathy, I require my wife. I forgive them for all the flowers that I have to watch wither and die, just as I watched you. I forgive the sympathy cards that remind me and the shrine they have built for you at the gravesite. You must forgive me for throwing the plates we got at our reception into the farm sink you picked out and watching them shatter last night. You must forgive me for falling apart into pieces the same as those plates, shattered. I forgive God for taking you, and I ask for forgiveness in thinking that your untimely departure was much too soon.

You see, sometimes in life, you do things not because you'd like to, not because it's convenient, and not even because it's the road less traveled. Sometimes, you do things because you know, deep down inside, it's going to pay off in the long run. You do some things for your well-being. You may eat organic, you may exercise every day, you may pray and meditate, or take a baby aspirin for heart health. You discover your purpose, enjoy your gifts, and exchange your gifts with others for your well-being. Just like these things, forgiveness is a part of your well-being. Include this in your daily journaling, laugh louder at yourself, and move forward. Because you will never realize your capacity to love, until you have cried for the person who hurt you the most. Forgive others, and you yourself shall be forgiven.

REMEMBER WHO YOU REALLY ARE

You are the mind. You are a part of the infinite reality and consciousness. All forms of medicine, all cures for dis-ease, all rearrangements of the biosphere, and proliferation of tissue resides in you. It has always resided in you and is waiting there, lying dormant for you to tap into its power.

Flow in the waves of energy, the pulsating rhythm of your life. Everything is ions moving, neurons firing, flesh sweating, and no empty space. Life itself is truly a dance. It's always jumping and changing beat, like the ropes turning and crashing against the concrete during a game of Double Dutch. Once you are connected, you can feel that pulse within life and jump in at the same pace. Whenever you couldn't hear our Father's voice before, it was because you weren't silent enough or still enough for long enough. Be still, so you can see the flashing red arrows that have always directed you onto your perfect path. Be quiet, and you can hear the channels of water that lead to your ocean of destiny. That feeling of fear is a constant reminder, pushing you forward in the small of your back. It is always there, simultaneously removing roadblocks out of your way, to create the path to your own true purpose.

You Are Alpha and Omega.

I've always been a feeling person. I am still, to this day, amazed at the fact that I and the soil are both the body of the universe. I adore how each and every thing in the time and space of this reality can choose to be whatever it wants to be. It is indeed, one of God's great gifts. So, I show gratitude to my treadmill for providing me with a mechanism for action so my body can run. I thank the water I drink for providing balance and composition within my tissues. I thank everything for taking on the form it has taken. Not only do I thank these things, but I thank myself, for in order for all the bonds of energy to be drawn to me, they could only be what I wanted for them to become.

You too are a master builder in your own life. You are your own observer. You are a part of the greater, infinite source, and we are all connected. In and out of time, experience, and matter, our total beings hold no greater or lesser weight. Therefore, try your best never to dismiss another's experience, point of view, or belief system. Everything has its unique value within a master builder's life.

If you are listening in on a conversation, part of that message is for you. If you are reading this book, it is intended for you to read. If you are driving by a car accident on the road, part of that experience is for you. It's like you're putting together a never-ending puzzle. Each day you have the opportunity to attach additional pieces to your puzzle, and those pieces can take on whatever shape you can imagine. All you have to do is speak it into existence, and then start building.

Anything spoken into existence is given life.

I recently spoke to one of my best friends who always said she didn't want children of her own. I think if I had asked her to watch my oldest daughter when she was little, my bestie would have cringed and "called Earl." (Earl is an acronym for vomit in the urban dictionary.) So, you can imagine my surprise when she started dating and eventually married a man with three kids. Through the marriage she has always been an awesome step-mother and treats her step-children as if they were her own. Over the years I asked her if having her own child was ever a thought in her mind, and she replied that it wasn't. She was content with the children God gave to her and didn't feel the need to have one of her own. I then received the news, that she had recently suffered two miscarriages. This news totally threw me off guard because we are best friends, yet she never indulged information that was so intimate to her.

Now, what's special about my friend is that she did not see the miscarriages as a complete tragedy. She was willing to hold herself accountable for what she spoke throughout her entire adult life. She stated that when she first found out that she was pregnant, she was terrified. As more and more time went on, she rationalized to herself, how she would be able to do it. Starting to see the joy in having a baby around the house though, was not enough to override all the discussions

67

with herself around the disappointment in having a baby throughout the years. She stood present in that experience and stated, "Well, I didn't really want a child in the first place." This statement was not wrong or right; I did not judge her. This was her truth, and she realized her power. I was more proud of her than anything, for acknowledging the strength in her words.

Once we recognize our power, we have infinite potential to create whatever it is we want and believe true to exist for ourselves. Through meditation I was able to tap into my existence outside of this current level of consciousness. It is my belief, that we are all a part of God, and in an attempt to be like God, who is all that ever was, ever is, and ever will be, we mimic all experience to imitate the reflection of our Father. We live our lives in observance. Our spiritual bodies sit in a completely different dimension watching as experiences play out in our physical bodies on earth. It watches to guide, to connect, and to experience life through you.

This physical body we walk around in is not infinite; the brain's function is, in essence, to keep us safe from harm. Our hearts are subject to emotional discomfort and joy, all in an attempt to be like our Father. To understand a universal love in our limited capacity, with the five senses as tools for experience, is what we've signed up for. But there is a much greater force that is guiding us. There is a much greater force pushing us towards what we need in order to experience life the way we want. And that is our higher self.

Each of our higher selves have been given an assignment. That assignment resides in this space while our true nature is beyond this realm and sits with the Father. This is why the Bible says, we are in the world, not of it (John 17:14-15.) If you were sent into this realm knowing fully who you are, and what you are capable of, what would be the purpose in that? You would no longer be able to experience life as a babe, because your eyes would be wide open. It would be equivalent to Adam and Eve, taking a bite of an apple. Once Eve bit into the apple from the Tree of Knowledge in the Garden of Eden, and then gave the apple to Adam to eat, they came into the realization that they were naked, and hid in the garden out of shame. If your eyes were opened, and you remembered your place amongst royalty, if you could remember that you were put here to experience yourself to be closer to God, if you could remember that you are the greatest creation that ever lived, would you then become ashamed of the life you've been living? Would you hide amongst your family and friends when the Father comes to see all the good works you've done? Would you be ashamed of the excuses you gave for why you couldn't reach your greatest potential?

When our eyes open spiritually from our heart song, and not from a place of logic or emotion, only then can we see the vast playground that has been set before us. We are truly children, and our happiness is the only thing that is wanted. However, when we get off course, hardships show up as a method to place us back on track. This place is where the stimulation and lessons of the universe come into play.

I know a doctor named Joy, an Obstetrics physician that absolutely loves her job. Joy always wanted to deliver babies for a living, as far back as she could remember. In her mind, there was nothing more precious than being a part of the welcoming committee when a new life came into the world. But when it came time to choose her career path in college, she considered becoming a nurse. Fear that her young children would be teenagers by the beginning of her career paralyzed her. She didn't want to spend the amount of time required by OB doctors, away from her girls. Fear of the unknown caused her to rationalize a career in which she wouldn't manifest at her highest potential. It was her mother who actually spoke vision back into her heart.

Joy's mom vividly remembered the countless toy stethoscopes broken by play throughout the years. Her daughter used up all the bandages in the house to cover her Barbie dolls and any other boo-boo she could find. There was literally nothing, but Barbie's auburn hair and green eyes peeking through her mummy-made ensemble. Joy's mother knew her daughter and the amount of care she would give to the children she would service. She knew that anyone who could swaddle a Popsicle stick and take its temperature was destined for greatness. Joy always saw the animate in the inanimate, and through imagination, grew congruent with the impossible. Her mother knew that as a nurse, though great and admirable, her daughter's life would not be lived in its fullest expression.

You see, there is something about the intuition of the parent that makes them say, "Go this way, not that way; do this thing, not that one. I'd rather see you happy, than not happy; you can have anything you want with hard work and discipline." There is a God-like consciousness to it, a celestial quality about it. A good mother or father can be the catalyst for their child's greatness. They are able to look inside of you and see the possibilities you were never able to see inside of yourself. And just by chance, Joy took the direction given by her mother and became a miracle doctor.

Throughout her residency, Joy became known for her ability to replicate what could only be described as supernatural phenomena. She could vigorously rub her hands on stillborn babies and life would return. Her colleagues simply thought she studied harder, when in fact with three children at home, she studied less. She fell asleep on top of her book in class, exhausted from working and going to school full-time. Her instructors kicked the leg of her seat and made jokes to the class about how she learned by "osmosis." She never was the most studious or the most time-efficient; things in school had always just come easily. She even contributed her own success to good "test-taking skills." No one really could put a finger on the special gift that she had, but everyone envied her ability. This point is where the utmost admiration and respect for her success in her career began.

Now, when a baby is born, there is a standard test that physicians and nurses utilize to determine how well the baby is doing. This is called the Apgar test, and is an acronym to assess the baby's Appearance, Pulse (heart rate), Grimace (facial expression), Activity (muscle tone), and Respirations. The test is usually given to the baby twice, one minute after birth, and then again in another five minutes. The scoring system is based on a one-to-ten scale; the higher the number, the better the baby's condition.

There came to a day in the young physician's life where Joy was to deliver a baby for a very close friend and her husband. The baby was part of a high-risk pregnancy, and the mother had been diagnosed with intrauterine growth restriction. The cord was also wrapped around the baby's neck three times. The medical team on the case decided it was time for the mother to be induced, since staying in the womb any longer might have increased the child's risk of death. Joy was the primary physician leading the delivery.

It was a muggy Sunday in April, and all day long the mother laid in bed, dilated at four centimeters. The nurses started an IV medication called Pitocin, which is meant to jumpstart contractions. At seven o'clock that night, after a day full without progress, Joy decided to break the woman's water and become ready for the welcoming. There were flameless candles lit around the room and the smell of vanilla was in the air.

The mother's contractions, after her water broke, came on fast and furious, stronger than anything she had ever felt before in her life. She honestly, felt as if she was going to die. She started to push, but knew that something was wrong, and that she shouldn't be pushing. The nurse had checked her progress only ten minutes previously, and she was still at four centimeters. She clung to the arm of her husband's shirt and screamed out loud for help. Yelling was the most rational thing she could think to do as she shook tremendously, unable to reach for her call light.

A nurse overheard the scream, without the husband leaving to ask for assistance. She ran into the room, looked under the white cotton sheet, and said aloud to the mother, "Well. Looks like we're going to have a baby." Dr. Joy, the mother's long-term friend and confidant, came rushing in the room. The ICU team stood by to assess and monitor the baby post-delivery. Within two minutes of pushing, the little boy entered the world. Within the first minute, the baby's first Apgar score was 3/10. He presented with a bluish skin tone, no crying, respirations and breathing were slow and shallow, and there was a low pulse rate with a limp response to the doctor's touch. Joy, turned to her resident physician to instruct on delivering the placenta, then rushed to the side of her friend's baby. She lifted the baby high into the air upside down and held him by his feet, vigorously stroking his back. She massaged him back and forth, back and forth. She tapped the child on the soles of his feet, laid him on his side, up against the warmth of the incubator blanket, and patted his bottom. The doctor literally worked this little boy over for the next eighteen minutes, stroking, massaging, tapping, patting. To the father, watching the boy being manipulated so vigorously by the physician, became almost unbearable. After five minutes, even he gave up hope of his own child's survival.

The ICU team stood around the doctor, questioning her practices. There was no suctioning, no compressions, no rescue breathing. Only two strong hands, one woman, one brave heart, and God. There was silence, and stroking, massaging, tapping, and patting, and on the 38th second of the 18th minute, that day, April 22, 2017, the baby let out the loudest cry the doctor had ever heard. Tears streamed down every face present in that room, all in thankfulness for this doctor's determination and perseverance to ensure that life would prevail.

Just like Dr. Joy, each of us has a higher calling on our life. When you remember that you are a spiritual being, that you have unique gifts within you, and that you are the observer of your own destiny, it brings you to the truth; that you can create whatever life you dream of. You can create children if you wish to, you can create the job that you want, and you can create things that have never been made before like airplanes that fly through the sky. You are the builder in your life, and your level of creativity depends on your belief of what exactly you are capable of.

The beginning and end of your greatest breakthrough, begins and ends inside of you.

When I think about this story, it reminds me of what I love most about my higher self, that it is this healer, nurturer, and guidance counselor in my life. It never gives up on me, like a mother, a doctor, it's knowing comes easily. Life sometimes motivates us with all sorts of situations, sprinkles us with all forms of fear and all kinds of harassment. It stimulates us to shape us and to keep us breathing, because one thing is for sure; if you're still breathing, you're still living. Life takes us, bends us, twists us, and stops us dead center in the path that we are running towards, turning us around saying, "No, baby, not that way." Amidst its greatness we are stroked, massaged, tapped, and patted, but sometimes those love taps don't feel good. Sometimes the sight of the hardships in your life can make you and others around you uncomfortable, because everyone, including you, has counted you out, but your guiding spirit has not.

The One above all just knows you're not done yet. The One knows how many times each child must endure the same lesson before he or she gets to the benefits. Above anything else, the Divine One knows once the lessons resonate and live, that your life is going to be "something else." Then you can run at full steam. Then you can experience true joy and forever love. When I finally realized the reasons behind all those times in which I felt like I couldn't breathe, I wondered to myself, who am I to second-guess those best practices of the Creator? All throughout my life I had clearly tried to get in the way of God's business.

After you get back to the place of remembering your spiritual self, I want you to remember who you are as your physical self. One of the most difficult things is tracing back who we were before the relationship with a romantic partner, before the birth of our kids, before the world told us to put our childhood dreams away in our back pocket. We have been taught that to love is to sacrifice, and we give so much of ourselves and invest our total being into other people. But you should always keep your life's work at the forefront. When we don't, we develop an emotional dependence on the other person. We look at ourselves in the mirror one day and no longer recognize who we are. So, whether you are in a dark place because of a breakup, a death in the family, or financial burden, I want you to remember who you are on this earth and what you want your legacy to look like.

I remembered who I was through writing. I remembered who I was through meditation. And most importantly I remembered who I was when I delved into my relationship with God. And the most perfect explanation of why I forgot who I was for so long, was that I was still looking for God outside of me. And when I stopped looking on the outside, I turned to the inside and found every answer to every question I ever needed.

To remember who you are, make a list of all the things you like to do, things that make you happy and induce a sense of euphoria. You may have to think back to your childhood; when was the last time you were truly happy? If it happens that you don't have any things or any memories, or that your happiness is considered something that may cause potential damage to yourself or others, you are actually in the greatest place of creation. You have the opportunity to start from scratch in exploring yourself and seeing all the new wonderful things that could bring joy into your life.

I had a couple of tricks that I remembered I could turn to, in hopes of dragging me out of the ditch of despair I dug for myself when going through my own depression. My personal tricks were singing, making jokes with my friends, and being around my family. However, sometimes when you are depressed, you no longer get enjoyment from the things that used to bring happiness. Then you feel like you're broken, or something must be wrong because you don't feel like the same person you used to be. What I did not know and I wish someone would have told me, was that I wasn't the person I used to be. I was growing into something more beautiful than I could have ever imagined.

Sometimes you just need some new experiences because your being is evolving. When you get a new job, you may need new clothes, right? So, when looking for new experiences that I needed to start enjoying my life all over again, I had to start with things that other people enjoyed. Not everything I did made my "forever list," but by trial and error you can determine and discover some new tools to be your better self.

I loved to discover new things, but what made my journey even more unique and fulfilling was to remember my innate gifts; the ones given to me from birth, the ones I didn't have to seek out because they were already there, the ones that came naturally. Some of my innate gifts were drawing, singing, design, and acting. And I loved exercising. I embraced these gifts more than the others, because they were what made me special. They continue to be what makes my story inside-out instead of outside-in. But what I didn't know was that I was a great writer. I never took the time out to sit down and write how I felt. When I wrote my story not only could I see it from a different point of view, but it caused me to fall in love with myself like never before. I also found an innate love for zip-lining which allowed me to release the control factor that I had held onto so tightly because of my perceived abandonment. And I had meditation, which I once thought was a waste of time, where I could quiet all the random thoughts in my mind, where I could see in my mind's eye things my physical eye could not see. My spirit was quiet, my nervous energy decreased and it allowed me to have greater clarity in my decision making. Now I have an arsenal of things, even greater than these, that I can go to when sadness starts to consume me. You must also now seek the tools God gave to you.

I would like you to sit at this time and physically write down all the things you enjoyed doing as a child. If you are going through a breakup, think back to what tools you used to help you get over the last one. Write down some things, that you have not tried yet.

If you're having a hard time thinking up with things, then download my FREE "How to Find My Happy" checklist at: www.breakingbravely.com

This download is an official bucket list for those in their darkest place. This list will remind you of the beauty in life and all the possibilities that await you. Figure out who you are and what you stand for today, in this life, because you are merging into a new beginning.

I want you to write out what you want your legacy to look like. What do you want your life to look like? One of the biggest things standing in our way is not fully choosing what we really want. Ask yourself the question, "What do I want to be remembered for?" The answer will help you to laser focus on the things that are most important to you. It's almost like someone in the beginning stages of dementia writing themselves a note in the darkness, in hopes that they will read it tomorrow to remember where they put their glasses, so they can see again. It may sometimes come in the form of sticky notes all over the bathroom mirror, but just seeing who you are, and what you represent is not enough. I want you to live the new you. I want you to breathe the new you. If you like to binge watch techie marathons on television, do what makes you the 2027 version of you. Then I want you to take action and do the things only you know that make you better.

Put yourself at the top of your daily priority list of what you need to take care of. I want you to say it out loud to yourself, and repeat it over and over again in the car. Write it daily in your journal and if you have to, record it and play it in your ears through your ear buds like a lullaby at night. "I like to go ice skating. I like to garden. I like to play video games." Whatever it is, speak out all the things that make you special. You're going to have to get desperate, hungry, and convicted enough to win your life back. You're going to have to believe in yourself before you are able to persuade other people to believe in you. We are here waiting on your brilliance and to see your gifts' magnificence. We are oohing and aahing, saying to ourselves, "I wonder what she/he's got?"

If you can't see the beauty in your gifts, or don't know what they might be, what do other people say about you? Has anyone ever told you that you would be good at something? Sometimes other people can see the gifts within us that we may not even be able to see for ourselves.

When you trace back through your life and remember who you were, what you liked, what you loved, before the hustle and bustle, you will fall deeper in love with yourself. You will become a "being in love," instead of looking to "be in love." When you reach this place, a level of self-love so surreal, don't allow anyone to enter into that space that could destroy your joy. If you even get the smallest inkling that there is a rift in your spiritual healing, put those people's names on the "love-from-a-distance" list. And when I say anyone, I mean anyone. It could be a brother, sister, mother, child, best friend, boyfriend, anybody. For who are you to place greater value on any other life than the one God gifted to you? How arrogant of you to sacrifice your needs for everyone else, when they didn't even ask for you. You are not needed everywhere all the time, but you are needed in one place all the time, and that place is within you.

When I could no longer look for what I needed in my spouse, my child, or my friend, I turned within.

Not only is it important to fall in love while getting to know yourself all over again, but start giving yourself the things that you have tried to give to everyone else. If your great at supporting your spouse's career goals, become even greater at supporting your own and putting those first. If you had a great idea for a new product that would change consumers' lives, make it; don't be so willing to give your ideas away at a discounted rate, and at the expense of your self-worth.

Now it is time to Journal, to fall in love with yourself all over again. In the next exercise, I want you to answer each question with three alternate endings. Then after you have answered all of the questions, I want you to go back and either highlight or circle only one response from each question that resonated with your soul. I want you to sit with yourself every day, either in a mirror or in a quiet place. If you are driving, you can also play your recording back to yourself in the car. Listen to the new conversation you have with yourself over the next 30 days. When you have a self-limiting belief, look in the mirror and repeat who you know yourself to be. Stand up for yourself, like you stood up for everyone else. Then go ahead into your day and be that change.

A Being in Love Exercise

Who Am I?

What is it that I want?

What did I want to be when I was a child?

Where were all of the places that I wanted to go?

What did I do best?

What are some things that other people have told me I do well?

What is the one thing I'd love to do most, that won't leave my spirit alone? What has stopped me from doing this thing?

The story I just told myself about what's been stopping me, is it true?

Who am I? What do I stand for? Who wouldn't love that?

I love all these unique things about me, but what makes me special?

God sprinkled little fragments of Himself into each one of us; which part of Dad did I get? Did I get His nose, His hair, His eyes? Did I get an unimaginable kindness in my heart, a tenacity in my spirit, or an appetite for humanity to thrive?

Ask yourself these questions, the answers will always appear. If you are still enough, if you are quiet enough, if you are willing to accept the answers. Write them down, say them out loud, record them into a voice recorder, then play your voice back and listen to who you are as if you two are meeting for the first time.

Be the Change

Being the change means living the life of your dreams as if it already existed; as if the moment of its presence is now. Being the change means extreme action and movements to improve your circumstances and well-being. It means doing the things you've been making up excuses to not do. Talk to yourself with a different language that you may not even believe. And grow into something that you have never seen before, because it is better, it is brighter, and it is your birthright. Being the change arrives and grows in the midst of being sick and tired of being sick and tired. It's asking for food on the corner because you have no choice. Being the change is being hungry. Hungry enough for anything better than your yesterday, and thirsty enough to run and drink at the well of your tomorrow.

In order to attract anything -- a partner with certain qualities and characteristics, a new job opportunity, financial wealth -- you have to be willing to play the part as if it's a fight for an Olympic medal. Just being invited to compete is not enough; we are going for the win, right? We want to live out our lives in our greatest capacity and within our greatest fulfillment.

When I move for anything I want present in my life, I move into the being of whatever that object is I want to attract. For example, in scrumptious detail, I created a list of qualities that I would like to be present in a romantic partner. I express gratitude for everything that is currently present in my life, and then set a subtle intention with visualization, creating the space for the partner with meditation, and enlisting extreme change, all while letting go of the need to know how it will all turn out. Instead of searching for these things to be afforded to me, I afford them to myself. I become that thing that I want the most. I become the partner I want to attract.

If you are looking for a man that always takes out the trash, guess what that means? You have to be willing to take out the trash! You could leave it there, rotting and smelling up the house, waiting for somebody else to come along and fix your problem. Or, you can fix your problem yourself. That way, when the help you want does come along, it will be a bonus and you can truly be grateful, because you know what it's like to do that job. If you continue not to be the person you'd wish to attract, you may still indeed attract someone who takes out the trash. You may start thinking it is a sign from God because that was what you prayed for. But, if it was not what you became, it is not for you, and you will always find it difficult to hold on to. I can also guarantee that a lot of other things that you may not like will come pre-packaged with those trash amenities. So, stop making excuses for why you can't get things done, unless you want to attract other people with that same list of excuses. On the receiving end, if you are looking for a partner to meditate with, then go the extra mile and buy an extra pillow. Make room for what you wish to attract and set up the space for your intention to manifest.

Create the space, then go hard or go home.

Space, the final frontier, is vital in order to be able to attract anything we seek. You must look at every area in your life and see if there is room for you to receive incoming blessings. You wouldn't keep ordering furniture off of the internet if you already had a furniture set in every room, unless you had some sort of addiction, right? So, let's get down to the basics.

It is impossible to attract the love of your life while doing things in your space, even if unintentional, that contradict his presence. If you want to attract your dream job, you must dress accordingly. Now I know that some of your current jobs may require a uniform, so my question for you then is, what is your attire like outside of that current situation? Do you go to the grocery store in pajama bottoms and flip flops? Now, I know that may be extreme, so let's go to our everyday commonality. Are you going to the store in ripped jeans and a dingy t-shirt? When you are out and about, enjoying your life, how lax are you in the way you dress and how you speak? If a multi-billionaire walked up to you, not knowing who you were, ready to engage in conversation, would you be ready? Are you wearing a bonnet or a wave cap on the top of your head in the middle of the day, as if you are ready for bed? If so, your dreams will also be asleep. Create the space in your wardrobe to attract new business opportunities.

Are you showing up in your life now as the person you admire or aspire to be? The infinite source cannot and likely will not grant your request for a seven-figure salary, when you walk around unprepared for the interview. This is why the majority of people are not the wealthiest or the most abundant. As long as you do what you've got to do to just "get by," you will only "get by."

When I say, be the change, I want you to go into beast mode and not least mode. After all, you wouldn't come to Thanksgiving dinner with a full belly. Animals do not go on fasts, they hunt when they are hungry. I want you to be on the hunt, for whatever it is you are hungry for. Sometimes our greatest blessings come from all the things we have to unlearn. Your cup cannot always be full and still expect blessings to pour in. God will never give you more than you can handle. Don't be the employee at your job, that is doing just enough. Don't be the person in your business putting in the least amount of time. BE HUNGRY for your vision, and come prepared to the table of life ready to feast.

When I worked as a home-care nurse, I was given the option to wear scrubs or business casual. I remember my boyfriend at the time telling me that I was always over-dressed for the occasion. Even though those scrubs were comfy, excellent at hiding problem areas, and took way less effort to plan what I would be wearing for the day, I refused to take the easy way out since I knew I needed an earthquake to shift and change careers. Deep down inside, the comfort was not what I wanted and definitely was not what I needed, so business casual was my choice. Dress the part of who you intend to be, not who you are expected to be.

I remember my father used to always tell me to go get washed up, put on clothes, and be presentable for the day ahead. He insisted on this even if all I planned on doing was sitting in the house all day, eating cereal, watching television, and maybe later in the day, walking twenty feet from the house to the studio to be creative. I remember dragging my feet like a toddler, and coming up with every kind of reason as to why this ritual was unnecessary. And then the child came out, and you may have heard some of these from your own children. It went a little something like this…

"Why make up my bed, if I'm just going to sleep in it again tonight and mess it up anyway? Why do I have to wash the dishes when I didn't dirty them? Why don't we just use paper plates and cups? Why do I have to dress up? I'm not trying to impress anybody. I don't like these people anyway. Why do I have to put on clothes, just to have nowhere to go?"

Don't we all do this in our lives to some extent? Don't most us say, if we didn't dirty the dishes then it's unfair to make us wash them? Why do all these things, as if our father is strolling through the house waiting until we sit down, just looking for something to tell us to get up and go do? I'll tell you why, because there is grace, favor, and omnipotent source in preparation. Because the calling on your life is bigger than what you imagined it to be, and it requires some discipline you didn't know you had to give. This is our parents' way of trying to get us to shift our paradigm. This is God's way as well.

The discipline given by your loving parents was not meant to hurt you, even though it may have. It was not meant to exert power or force; it was not meant to demean you. It was there as guidance to show you how to discipline yourself in your own adult life, when no one is around to make you. The discipline to live intentionally, to have the life you want, lies within these smaller moments. If you want to live in a clean environment, you need to keep your current environment clean. You will never have enough money to hire a maid to do it for you, or if you do hire a maid you cannot fully appreciate the services he or she provides. So, go big in all of your efforts, or just give up now and go home.

When I do "Go Hard or Go Home" exercises in my own life, I bet no one can do it like me. And do you know what the best part is? No one can do it like you. Show up for yourself in your life. To attract love, first you must fall in love with yourself. Myself and I go on dates together. I buy birthday and Christmas gifts and wrap them and hide them, then feel surprised and gracious when I open them, like I haven't the slightest idea where they came from! When I sit down for dinner, I may have the waiter or waitress leave an extra place setting to create room for the friend or romantic partner God is sending to be present in my life. I can't even tell you how many times I've visited the bookstore and envisioned my book signings, the amount of people showing up to say thank you, and the stationary that comes personalized with each copy. Make the visualization for your dream so real, even if you have to stand in the middle of that house you want and rub on the granite while the realtor looks at you like you have lost your mind. Go to the extreme to touch, feel, smell, and see your dreams coming true.

Officially, I want my ladies to get this deep down in your soul and walk as wives choosing their husbands… That empty space on one side of the bed is not for you and definitely NOT for your kids! It's hard for God to send your soulmate when you have taken up all the room. Even when you are single, unless you are intentionally single, make room. Because one of the most awkward things after finally getting the love of your life, is having to deal with the crying babies at your bedroom door. That place was not meant for them in the first place. You drew them close to make yourself feel better.

Most of us enter into a place where we feel lonely, because we lose sight of what we are here for. You get to choose whoever you want to be, everything that you wish to accomplish, and how you're going to go about getting the things you desire. Once you remember who you are; an observable being, you get to walk like it, and talk like it. You get to go hard or go home. Life is full of new experiences in which we can take comfort in enjoying, when we remember the old experiences. Your being is always evolving. Don't feel a loss of identity if you have tied who you are to the last 20-30 years of your life. Look at all the years ahead of you. And you can rest assured in the knowing that you can make those years mean anything, say anything, or be anything that you want them to.

THE POWER OF RELEASING CONTROL

If there was a round table, where all the emotions came and had Sunday brunch over tea and cucumber sandwiches, I am almost 400% sure there would be assigned seating. Happiness doesn't want to sit next to Bitterness. Hurt runs around the table eager to slap everyone in the back of the head and externalize its pain. And if you look closely, buddied up whispering in the ear of Abandonment is Control. Seated at the table is God, not acting as interference, but behaving as an observer. Just like in homeroom at school, we attempt to sit with the familiar, those we are used to, and rarely seek a new group of friends. Sometimes it is made to seem as if our loyalty is discredited if we don't sit amongst the dysfunctional. We assign our own seating and this seating presides at the table of our heart.

Control is the bestie that begins to fight all of Abandonment's battles. It operates as a big brother or sister and serves out of fear, to protect us from getting hurt. Control is similar to the brain's function in its ability to keep us safe. However, keeping us safe also inhibits us from reaching our maximum potential in relationships, in physical health, within career goals, and in finances.

This "acting out" emotion is so subtle and quiet at times, that we don't even recognize its presence. It is a defense mechanism operating from previous fear-based beliefs and robbing you of a more carefree and fulfilling life. Control can lie and make you believe that manipulation is a loving behavior, but it is not. To love is to simply let people be as they are. With control, we want to tweak or change other people into who we think would be better for us. People who feel controlled, if they have a healthy self-conviction, will generally behave as a caged animal. They will try anything to get away, even if it means cutting off their own foot to be free of your shackle.

Control can be the equivalent to a self-inflicted natural disaster. It will halt your ability to be vulnerable; therefore connecting with others and building sustainable intimate relationships will become a challenge. In an attempt to "never be abandoned again," we precipitate those same experiences and further become abandoned by others. Since we are adults, we now have a choice in experiencing how others will treat us.

We did not choose our experiences as children, it was given to us. But as adults, we now can put up walls and build a shelter or a fort, with weaponry set out to destroy anything that comes close, that is not on our terms. This weaponry also leaves us isolated, in a world that is fully engaged and waiting for us to come outside and play.

The only person you can or ever will be able to have control over is Yourself.

What other people say, or how they behave, or how they are, can only be transformed if that is a decision they choose to make. If they don't see a higher level of consciousness, it is not your job to understand why. Your commitment is to yourself and you alone. Do not expect someone else to see value in what God has instilled within you. People wouldn't believe wind was real if they didn't feel it. Sometimes other individuals are not, in their current life journey, ready to fully receive acceptance of a particular lesson that you have already learned. This reason is also why we cannot base our happiness off of things external of ourselves. Only your lessons are based on your time, their lessons are not.

We must learn to love people within their journey, instead of grabbing the hands of everyone around us and dragging them to our finish line. If you look back, their knees will become bloody, their clothes tattered and worn, and their spirit tired; they will just want you to let them go. By holding on to others, you also slow yourself down in the process. You could finish your race so much sooner without the extra baggage. Stop attempting to rearrange the outcome of other's lives around you. Transform your life, and other's lives will follow.

Protection in the absence of danger is like pulling the latch on a fire extinguisher when there is no fire present. You stand still, waiting to fight a fire when there is not even a hint of smoke. When you distract yourself with what could happen, you are not really a part of what is happening. Protection causes us to live from a place of fear. Any fruit produced from a tree of fear will not yield sufficient nutrition. Just because you survive in fear does not mean you live in freedom. And trying to control the world around us, is always an inside job. Dissonance comes into play, so we don't understand how to connect back to our internal guidance system and build in the spiritual realm.

Release Control of Your Children

With our children, have you ever noticed that instead of allowing them to be who they are, most adults drive them to be what they think will provide the children the highest level of happiness and comfort in their adult lives? Now, the intention is good, however when we are not able to exercise control in our own lives, it often bleeds over into theirs, and this is where we bathe them in our own self-lack and deficit. We often tell them to sit and be quiet instead of discovering why they move or listening to what they talk about. Because sometimes, to be honest, the noise and movement gets on our nerves. We have so much going on in our own lives that by the time we get home, we just want a minute alone to relax. It is not up to your children to create these moments for you or to be reprimanded when you do not create the time and space for yourself.

Just think about how many sports and dance classes we sign these tots up for. I, by the way, love sports and dance, but I am not into extracurricular activities that my children cannot express their best self at. How many people do you know, that complain about the drive time, the hopping and the running, but can't wait to sit in the bleachers screaming, or to slap a soccer mom sticker on the back of their car? Could we not be utilizing this time and space to create the life of our dreams? If we put as much attention into our personal dreams as we do into our children, then we could live a life of our own and not piggyback off of theirs. That's what I intend for my children, to be an example of how mommy did it, so they have the tools to create their own version of success. A safe place to play full out, where we embrace disappointments and setbacks, then we get right back up. I want for my children to look at mom and say, "Now, that's how you get back up," and to see perseverance pay off. I want them to see me pursue my own happiness. And I want to be present, so I don't miss their pursuit, or just tack on what mommy decided was best on the menu.

Our molding, and attempting to shape their destiny, is all about us, because quite frankly, we like to hear, "job well done." We like to brag about how our child is more talented or smarter than the others. It gives us a sense of accomplishment, right? The question I pose is, what is your perception of a "job well done?" Whose gauge of accomplishment are we measuring against? The more conscious you are of your child's individualism, the more able you will be okay when they leave the home.

Empty nest syndrome, I believe, is a sadness for the lost time you spent not dwelling in your own experience and dreams, because you chose someone external of you, your children, to fill that void. And most would give the advice, that if you find yourself a new buck to a single-parent household, to focus all of your energy on your children, to get through the upcoming years. But providing them with security and safety requires focusing on your individual growth. If mommy or daddy is spiritually whole, the children will be a mirrored reflection of that wholeness.

Ask yourself, is my own life as fulfilling as the one I am attempting to create for my children?

If your life is one that is empty, and deep-down unfulfilling, your children will pick up the spirit of being unfulfilled, even if it might not be manifested until their young adult years. I sometimes think, the emotional bond we have with our children, is because unwillingly, they are the only ones we can exert that much control over. Because what happens when they are at their most independent thinking stages, and they come to a place where they try to have some control over their destiny? We start throwing out the "T" words! The two T words that are most prevalent, and what I believe are urban legends, are the Terrible Two's and the Troubled Teens. These are another set of passed-on beliefs that our parents placed upon us, and now we expect it from our own kids. We have the choice to either believe in them or to pass on a belief to them and their children that no longer serves our purpose.

You should see the looks, and hear the grunts of discomfort when I tell people I have three girls. Very seldom, do I hear positive things. Most of the time people grab anything close and look at me, expecting me to take cover as well. It would seem as if the storm of the century is brewing with that much estrogen in one household. The comments are especially trying when they come from my own mother. I have to constantly remind myself of what I choose for my own beliefs and how those beliefs will determine my experience.

The stories of a teenager's life can only be told from their own and their parents' perspectives. Even into adulthood my perception changed, but the experiences are what remain constant. Sometimes parents seem to have selective memory into the things that their children did wrong. And some people believe the old, "You do it, because I said so, and I'm the parent," model worked on them, but did it?

Between 11 and 12 years old, my oldest daughter became almost unrecognizable. All of a sudden, she changed, and it was frightening for me, because she didn't seem like the same person. I held onto the idea of wanting to know in advance who she would become. I expected a constantly evolving being to remain the same. I hoped that the vision of what I always thought my daughter would be, and her vision for what she wanted to be, would magically align with the stars and produce clarity for me. But suddenly, when I asked her a question, instead of getting the straight answer I had been used to, she required a clarification of my initial question. Not only did she require a clarification, but now I was put on the spot to provide an explanation for why I even asked her a question in the first place. I thought my trump card would be, "Because I said so," or "Because I pushed you out," or "Because I provided you with 23 of your chromosomes." But even though she would answer the question or perform the task I asked, this challenge only created more distance between us.

The relationship that was present in my own home, was similar to that of a disgruntled employee. You know, the one that cares nothing about a vision statement or methods for good customer service. The one that shows up late for work, and only comes for the paycheck. My daughter walked through the home angry, getting into screaming matches with her younger siblings for every little thing they did that annoyed her. Well, guess who she learned that from? She said how much she hated them, and that our time before them was better, because she had more of me to herself. She externalized her pain onto her sisters and her mother. The hole that was left there was from a subconscious hole within myself. She stated how much she hated other people in the world around her, and at one point, called her father to come pick her up so she could go live with him. In an attempt to gain control of an already uncontrollable situation, I told her to leave. I was okay with her leaving because then it was my choice, she made the decision but still required my permission. I could have said no, but actually what I discovered was that her leaving would have been my failure. I then discovered what led to our disconnect in the first place.

In my mother's household, when she was small, there was no say-so from the children. To her, children were not beings that had voices, and if they did it would be, "spanked out of them." I chose not to raise my children this way, but still found myself saying the things and acting out in ways exactly like those of my mother. I had not patched the hole in my life boat from the emotional termites she set free, and now those termites had babies and generations of holes that ate their way into the solid hearts of my children. Intentionally raising children allows you to acknowledge where your self-limiting growth in parenting stems from and assists you in shifting into a parental role that best serves you and your individual circumstance.

So, I began to change how I interacted with my daughter. I did not take her to counseling, because she was not the one who needed it. I continued to bust into her room unannounced most of the time, but started to knock when I remembered, since this is what she requested. I let her shave the sides of her head, with her father's support. I allowed her more freedom and released the determination to control and manipulate her every move. I created a safe environment for her metamorphosis.

The most substantial shift that happened within our relationship came when I started feeling and treating myself differently. You see, others around you, including your children, watch you to determine what you'll accept, and how they will behave to be present in your life. If you feel and treat yourself as a failure or as worthless, others will take their cues from you and treat you as such, including your children.

Once an intentional change happened within me, including remembering who I was, finding my purpose, and becoming expansive with inner joy, I was no longer stressed. I no longer required the need of external things for my happiness. Stress was no longer on the menu; I beamed from the inside out. I stopped worrying about how my child would turn out. You cannot set subtle intention for others but you can set subtle intention in how you wish to interact, and then let go of the end result. While being present, I became a happier woman; therefore, she could only become a happier child.

Our children, like every other person, event, and circumstance around us, are mirrors into our spiritual wholeness, reflecting all the best things or all the broken things within ourselves. Each child represents a different part of yourself and your partner, and serves as an external reminder that to treat them with empathy, understanding, and love while allowing for growth, is to treat yourself to those same gifts. They also teach us which areas in our beings we could be a little more loving and attentive to.

Once I changed my inner self, my child became a reflection of that. I remember the first time I came home from work while the girls were on spring break, and walked into a home where the girls were laughing instead of arguing. There my oldest daughter was wrestling with her two younger sisters, tickling them behind their chubby knees, playing games, and by the end of the night, she and my middle daughter shared a bed. They slept together for the next couple of nights, and it was like no issue between them had ever existed. She received, a week or two later, her first "all-A" report card, and was incredibly excited.

She continued to dress and style her hair the way she deemed appropriate, but something became evidently present in her being that had not been there before. She was happy, as happy as I had seen her in years, and it became ever so present in her outpouring of affection, laughter, and ability to treat others kindly. All of a sudden, she wanted to be closer. She wanted more hugs and even an occasional kiss. She even began asking if I would let her cuddle up at night in my bed, however since we were both a size 9.5 women's' shoe, I figured to have a little bit more room on the couch would be more appropriate. Baby steps!

Remember, you will be a novice at not ruling control out of force, but managing it with good leadership skills with your kids. One hundred eighty degrees of change will not occur overnight. In my situation in particular, nothing came overnight or all of a sudden, but it all came together, "on purpose." I ended up having a better relationship with my daughter, her attitude has significantly improved, and her teachers at school think she's the best thing since sliced bread. I think she's the best thing too. It was my responsibility to let go of the little girl I knew and embrace her transition into young womanhood. The added bonus was that my release of trying to control the situation came with increased spiritual awareness for myself and the memory that I came from a place that was grounded in love.

Our next generation will sweep the face of the planet with more free thinking and self-accountability than any other generation before them. This is the generation of dreamers and conscious master builders.

So, When We Don't Have Kids, Who Else Do We Control?

Another form of control that can show up in our lives is in the interruption of intimate relationships. After the separation from my girls' father, I felt like I had wasted a lot of my youth and time. I mean, here I was with a man for eleven years that I didn't even get married to. Yes, we got engaged a couple of times, and there was one time I called off our wedding two weeks before the guests were to arrive, but I had my reasons. If we would have gotten married, it would have ended in a divorce, and I never wanted to get married if that possibility was so present within my mind and my heart space. After our relationship ended, I panicked at the story I would have to tell when the men I dated would ask. I felt like a scarlet letter had been branded on my forehead, a single, big red "S," and that did not stand for Stacie! I was once again single and terrified of the whole experience.

It just so happened that my next fiancé had no children of his own and loved the girls and I very much, to the best of his ability. Still, since I hadn't fully forgiven the hurt of my past, I came into this relationship operating from pieces of hurt, neglect, and abandonment, so I attempted to control the outcome and timeline of our relationship. This, ladies and gentlemen, is what is referred to as "baggage." At the doorstep to a new relationship, please do a bag-check at the door, because in my life today, I no longer even bring a carry-on.

Now I understand the concept that after the completion of a relationship, it is important to get clear on the things that you want and do not want from a potential partner. However, if your don't-wants continue to show up, after you've repeatedly, in a dignified manner, requested what you need to feel secure, yet you have to continue to argue about it, defending your stance on the situation, or agreeing to behave the way the other person wants you to, only to get what you want, then control and manipulation are at work in the relationship. When you are present in who you are, your authenticity, and what you are, there is no need to defend your requests for what you want. You have nothing to be ashamed of. Therefore, if someone is not in agreement with giving you what you need, you have the choice to not make space for that person who no longer serves your purpose.

We can only act accordingly to how others want the relationship to go, but only for so long, especially if our desires in a relationship are within a core belief or moral that we simply cannot budge on. Once the ego realizes that we are abandoning a part of ourselves, our perfect God-given being, created uniquely to serve others, it self-sabotages the relationship. The inner child is not always in control, but it becomes enraged and furious when you begin to give up the essence of who you are in exchange for another person to stay in a relationship. When your inner child feels neglected, it will throw tantrums all over your external world, friends, and relationships. Saying or doing things to preserve the peace, avoid confrontation, and to keep another being present in any capacity is an act of desperation. Control comes into the picture, when we assume that our words, actions, or new-found beliefs will eventually mold them, like Jell-o, into the person we "need" them to be. Eventually, even if we do win the game, so to speak, it was not won with merit or integrity, and the dissolution of that relationship will come down the pipeline. We should be all ready and everything we "need," when entering into a relationship. Your partner is only the icing on your cake of greatness.

Here are some encouraging affirmations which allowed me to move past a place where I felt as if I didn't get what I wanted, I was a failure, and I had lost. I would like you to say these affirmations if there has been someone, a situation, a job, or a person that you have been trying to hold on to.

Release Affirmations

People have a right to change their minds and choose their experiences including me. I too have the right to come and go as I please.

What people do, how they act, who they love, has nothing to do with me and everything to do with them.

My job is not to prove my worth.

To love is to release; letting go requires more strength than holding on to something that God is trying to take away.

During my younger adult years, I became extremely comfortable at telling others what I needed in a relationship, but what I was not comfortable with was the lack of their presence. Relationships are most definitely a balance of energy that take two whole people. You are not in a relationship to complete one another, you alone, are already complete. If you go outward, seeking your "better half," you are only half a person, and therefore life will send you, by certified mail, another whose cup is only half-full. It is much more difficult trying to grow together with someone else before doing the work on your hurt alone. If you were not taught how to love, you cannot expect the other person to teach you that. You should learn this lesson, so that you have that tool to offer, so you are careful not to hurt others. To be unintentional is intentional, and within growth in a relationship, you can actually grow apart and learn of something different you may desire. You can grow to become irrationally co-dependent, even when love "hurts," or continue to be present but indecisive, and grow resentful.

Knowing your purpose and discovering what you want in your life is your job, before meeting a life-partner. If your spiritual tank is not full, you are more likely to blame problems, areas of discontent, and feelings of unhappiness on the other person. And most hurtful of all, we attach shame, regret, and an overwhelming lack of accomplishment to relationships that we were not ready to enter in the first place. We attack the easiest, most reliable, and uninhibited source that is closest to us, which oftentimes is our spouse. This is why we hurt the ones that are the closest to us; it requires the least amount of work to blame the person directly in front of you.

Through Control, What is it that You are Seeking?

We want to know that there's going to be a pot of gold at the end of the relationship rainbow. If we work really hard, we want something tangible to show off our good works. When we go to school and study diligently, we expect an A and to see our name on the Dean's List, along with flowers and medals and any other form of recognition that we can get. We would like to know what the rate of return will be on our investment, and whether to keep depositing funds into that account, because at this point in our lives, most of our accounts are on auto-deposit but remain bankrupt. We want to know that when we walk into our supervisor's office that we will get the raise we deserve at the rate we've asked for. But relationships, with other people involved, do not work in this manner. You take a risk when consistently there is another person present within your space to bump into and help to round out those sharp edges you've grown so accustomed to. But if you make the intentional choice to grow, shape-shift, and conform without abandoning yourself, with empathy for yourself and others, the love you discover is one of the most amazing, uninhibited feelings in the whole world.

INTENTIONAL FAITH

Move forward in your purpose, even when that means standing alone

Understand that you might not be able to take everyone along with you into the journey of your success. Firstly, your vision of success is as unique to you as you are to the world, and therefore someone can share in it or be of it, but only you can live it and breathe it into existence. Secondly, your vision was given to you as an assignment from God. Do not continue to walk through life attempting to cheat off other people's test papers or paying someone else to do your homework. You must to do the work to receive the grace.

So, in that regard, become settled with the thought, held near to your bosom, that you may have to walk your vision to the finish line alone. I want for you to become graceful with that walk. Your stride has to take on good form. The thought of the journey must no longer make both eyes well up with big crocodile tears. The vision that was given to you is for you, and for you alone. There will be people along the way that can see it, there will be people that talk about it, there will be people that doubt your path, but the people who stay close are the ones who believe in the mission, not the man.

Many of us are feeling people, but some of us have to be in the field of another's energy that aligns with our own to speak their language and understand the passion behind their dreams. For me personally, I don't need to be in your shoes, to be empathetic towards your struggle. I am so intertwined in my connection with others, I can feel it. That's what we call being, "in tune," or better yet, tuning into the tune within.

Our bodies function a lot like radios and sometimes we have just forgotten how to find the right station. Every day we tune into the people who will allow us to express our faith in the unseen. There is an undercurrent to our interaction with one another, an energy felt, but unheard. Every now and then, I come across a genre of music I might not prefer, I observe it and then I turn the station and move on. This same rule applies when meeting people who don't pour possibility into my spirit. I observe them, and then I move on.

We are built to sing with each other's vibrations in a multitude of harmonies and on a plethora of platforms. So, it is easy to believe in others without knowing them personally. You may not care for their music, but empathy allows you to understand their method. You should want people to succeed. Their version of success is also a part of your own. For you cannot fully connect with the internal of yourself without knowing the in's and outs of what's external of yourself.

However, you are the master of your destiny. We want everyone come along on our journey because we operate at a completely different level with human interaction, but that does not necessarily mean other beings need to be around. It is actually when you become consistent in your faith, when you are comfortable carrying the torch and not looking back to see who's behind you, that is when you reach your destination. And when you arrive, there will be people, the ones put there by God to cheer you on. We must try not to put much thought on why the people we choose do not choose us, but instead trust the creator, for life gives us exactly what we need.

When you meet those people, the ones that look into you and see a greater possibility than you had ever seen for yourself; the ones that you go to an event with and they run around telling everyone who you are before you even arrive. The ones that spend all night working on a project for you, and then in the morning accept the long laundry list of things you don't approve of with ease and calm; when you find these people, hold them close. Nurture these relationships, these earth angels. You will need them to remind you of your faith when you begin running to chase down your dream.

When I first started walking my journey in 2016, I had a list of things I was going to accomplish intentionally. Yet, when my intentions started to take shape around me, I became afraid. All the writing, planning, and strategy suddenly made what once seemed unattainable to me, real. And it was this realness that had scared me into complacency for so many years. The manifestation of things I wanted frightened me even more, because I never had experienced them before. It's kind of like having a lamp and rubbing it, and then realizing there is a genie inside. Now you have to really be clear on what you want. When there was no genie, you never even thought you had a chance of making your dreams come true, so you never had to focus. I started to focus on mastering different areas of my life, so that I wouldn't arrive at my destiny and sabotage myself with old thought patterns and beliefs.

See, before I was an author, a speaker, and a coach, I was a nurse. Before I was a nurse I was a customer service representative. And before I worked customer service, I was a manager. Before I was a manger, I was a mother. Before I was a mother, I was a woman. And before I was a woman, I was a girl. When I was a girl every piece of life that I was to live already existed within me. But all of these roles had to be mastered, otherwise life wouldn't allow me to move forward into my destiny.

We are all constantly trying to figure out how to master each area of our lives, so we can graduate, so we can transform, and so we can move forward to the next level. This is why I now offer my Personal Development Coaching Program. The program was especially important to me in helping me to remove my own limiting beliefs. I knew I didn't want to chase a dream that one day I would be unable to handle. And I was tired of attracting the same situation over and over again, from my relationship with money, to men, to my career. My life was on repeat. I know my purpose is not over however, because I am still here. I know I have not mastered an area when I feel stuck and just don't know what the next move is. So be intentional with your investment in yourself, and everything you do with faith that is good for yourself will flourish. Personal Development was one of the best investments I ever made.

When I was a manager, I learned how to build a team. I discovered how to set goals with action steps and how to hold people accountable. I could even train the heck out of new employees to meet the company's agenda. But what I couldn't do, was make my team love me. I sat at home with a corrective action slip in front of me, and came up with three or four different ways to present the paperwork while talking to myself in the mirror. No matter, which method I chose, or what non-threatening color I wore to work that day, my team followed me by fright and not by conviction. They didn't willingly come along to play, focused on how great a job we could do; they came for a check and did what I said, because that was along the path to getting their bills paid. I was a manager, but I was not a leader. And the fear wasn't because I was a leader who didn't lead by example, it was that I never mastered the art of how to communicate my needs and have tough conversations, while leaving people's dignity intact.

My passion there as a manager was to do a good job, to receive the praise of my leaders, to meet the goals and break the numbers, but it was never for my own self-worth. There was a need to provide for my family, but not for my soul. There was a disconnection between the woman I was, and who I was meant to be. Sometimes when you don't feel well, when nothing is going the way you think it should, when you don't have a "clear" picture, you may need to check your connection.

What I received wholeheartedly through my management career were some solid truths that I use to this day. For one, every success before ours left a recipe for how it was created, A Blueprint. If you want this, you do that; all we need to do is to tap into and allow that recipe to stretch us. The strategy for your life you came into this world with is not something that is given to you; it is something already within you. It comes with a feeling, a deep-rooted instinct that moves you towards the things you love. But to get there means believing in the impossible, dreaming the unimaginable, and running for what lies beyond the finish line when everyone else has stopped. Just like for an organization, you already have the game plan inside of you, but are you willing to implement the steps?

We cannot be settled in who we have always been and expect to receive the type of spiritual growth we yearn for. Where we are trying to go may stretch us so drastically that we start to develop body distortion issues. So instead, we stay close to who we recognize in the mirror. That beaten woman may be broken, but I know that face. That divorced man may be heartbroken, but I know that heart. We stay quiet. We try not to draw too much attention. We gather in nooks and crannies and talk about the things that frighten us. We shrink into the commonality of it all. But your faith will pull you away from that mirror. Your faith will drag you away from the fun house kicking and screaming into the new high-definition vision for yourself.

Secondly, through my management training, I learned about setting goals, the more tangible the better. There is always "the goal," then action steps, a vision statement, resources needed, and a timeline. Oh my, a timeline! I realized I never gave myself a timeline for achieving my goals. The thing about timelines is that they make the goal become real. Telling other people about your dream allows you to have other people to hold you accountable for the things you say you are going to do.

I told myself that I was willing to do whatever it took to get to my goal. My personal goals were to complete this very book and have it published, meet the mentors I had on my vision board, travel more, follow my financial plan for bringing in more revenue, and hire a coach.

But what I think is deep down in most of our guts is the voice saying, "I am willing to do anything, but if I can get there by trying to take the easy way out, I'd be okay with that along the way."

When life started taking shape and gave me the things I wanted, it was super uncomfortable in the beginning. I started to question whether I should want those things in the first place, and whether they were meant for me. The only person I could express my true feelings to was one of my nearest spiritual sisters. I spoke of how fear paralyzed me in at moments. A lack of faith can have us take a seat of complacency if we allow it to, so I openly expressed, I was scared! At that moment it would have been easier to settle back into the expectancy of others and my old self. I knew the end result of my work for so long in my life, that walking purely by faith seemed irresponsible. But one thing had changed, I was not old, everything about me and in me was NEW, and I could only expect circumstances, places, events, and people around me to mirror that change. That's one of the greatest gifts of all we have at our fingertips. Once you change yourself you can change the world.

Right next to that question of whether or not I deserved what I had asked for, sat the question of what my legacy would be. What was it I wanted to be remembered for? With each new decision I shaped this legacy. I became hypersensitive to this truth. I was developing the way my children would talk about me and how they would function as adults. I was forming what I thought of myself and whether I really loved myself as much as I said I did. I was crafting a bigger future, larger than I could imagine. The question that remained was, was I ready? And if I wasn't ready, why did I ask for the life of my dreams in the first place?

We ask for things in life we want all the time without having any idea of what we may have to sacrifice, who we may have to leave behind, who we may have to become, or what we may have to quit sooner than expected, to become who we yearn to be. I was the first person I tested my theory on; the theory of sight in the unseen and breaking bravely into my best life.

Frankly, I was very resistant to coaching others on what breaking bravely really means. This process was special and it was mine, but the demand grew larger as more and more people saw me showing up in my own special greatness. God allowed me to see how arrogant I had become. I wasn't allowing anyone else in on my secrets to success. They saw in me how great their lives could be, but I thought they didn't need me until my own life was completely turned around. Yet, people showed up for the journey, not the polished product. And then, in every way, it seemed that my experience, not my education, would make me the most qualified for the position I asked for. One thing the Universe does not care about, is your level of experience. The greater being will promote the maid to a position higher than the warrior, because of *who* she knows, not *what* she knows. This realization became the rocket fuel for my success as a Best-Selling Author. I learned people showed up for the book, but they also arrived for me and the feeling I pushed into a room. What I came to learn during the journey is that the blessings fall within your doing.

I have seen people with master's, law, and doctorate degrees living in poverty. I have seen the ending place for multiple people, from all walks of life, and they all end up the same. Through my career in nursing, I visited the homes, the assisted living facilities, and the hospitals of your loved ones. I talked with thousands of elderly patients about their lives, what they thought worked well, and what they would do differently. Some of those people maybe had a little more square-footage, or a couple more diamonds around their necks, but they still met the same fate despite their level of experience or what they did for a living. I've seen the high and mighty with Alzheimer's, like the woman, who was a stay-at-home mother, yet forgot the names of all her children. I have looked upon the faces of individuals riddled with mental illness, as if alternate spirits had taken over their body. And I've also seen the owner of adult foster care homes, telling our mothers and fathers, uncles and cousins, brothers and sisters to EAT! "It will keep up your strength," they say, as they pat them on the back and add thickener to their liquids and puree their meat, feeding them as if they were cattle. I wonder if we would still kill livestock if we could collect a check from Medicare every month to keep them alive.

I have seen people work for 30 years, for someone else's dream, then watch it break down their bodies and spirits. I watched those people turn into smokers, and the anxiety led to sunken eye spaces, yellowed teeth, thinning hair, bulged discs in their backs, thin bones, and depression. And the one theme that remained consistent is that each of those people admired faith. Not everyday faith, like God will provide you with what you can handle, but falling off the cliff faith in hopes someone will catch you. Crashing down from running so hard, getting back up with bloody knees, and picking up the pace kind of faith. The, I can't get any sleep because I'm trying to trigger my water to break so my body can go into labor, and I can birth the dream that is placed within me kind of faith. We are all headed to the same place, but how exciting would it be if your faith was radical along the way?

I made a choice that if I had to deal with so much uncertainty, an unsolicited amount of stress to live out a dream, that it would at the very least be a dream of my own. Not a dream by default on whatever course life chose to give me. I set an intention to become the chooser in all areas of my life. You can choose for your life as well. You can choose where you work; you can choose how you allocate your time; you can choose what's important and what's not important; you can choose who you marry. You can choose your life. The very best thing about becoming the chooser is that then you have the options. Once you have options you are no longer operating from a field of deficit. You are no longer sitting around waiting to be chosen. You are the observer, and you have the power.

I became the chooser of my worth, the chooser of my career, the chooser of my love-ships, the chooser and developer of my happiness. I chose to run the race for myself and not for the sake of others. So then, what others thought about me didn't matter so much anymore. What mattered was whether I could like and love and live with myself. All other likes and loves and living-withs became extra credit.

I remember preparing for a meeting with my investor a couple months after setting my latest life invention into creation, to say some things that I've never said before, to, do some things I had never done before. I chose to walk by faith. I had nothing to lose because everything else I tried in the past had either left me broken or stuck, both of which were like death because I wasn't living up to my fullest potential. This meeting was one of the first events that propelled me into a quantum leap.

The new director of my department explained to me that at every job she held previously, she did not get compensated for the work that she had to do at home. Not only was she not compensated, she expected me to do the same. Since dysfunction had become her norm, she looked to bring others to that same level of dysfunction.

Put people in a position of power and they will show you who they are.

It never occurred to her that she had been taken advantage of. Sometimes people can be taken advantage of for so long, by so many people, that they function within the deficit. Not only do they function, they externalize their pain onto others. I asked myself, for this woman, when did she start becoming unimportant? I felt empathy for the hole she carried inside. Her outside appearance mirrored those same character traits, but she was special and I loved her for it. The thing about loving someone because they are special is that nobody likes people who like them more than they do themselves, and she clearly didn't know how to like herself.

Now, since the beginning of my resurrection, the most important piece of my legacy and my brand is believing in what you stand for. For me, I most truly believe in God first and then myself. My value was not determined by this director, nor is it determined by any other woman or man external of me. My value was not even decided by the owner of the company, and giving away my time without compensation was something I was not willing to do. Not only was I unwilling, but unable. It would have made me sick, smoking, gaining weight, with yellow teeth, thinning hair. It would have meant wrinkles and bags under my eyes. An attempt to quench the thirst of sleep through a spirit in a constant state of lethargy. It would have meant handing over my life, it would have "killed me." I wonder how many of us say yes to what the boss tells us to do, just because we've been conditioned to say yes.

I however, could not and would not say yes. I had made up my mind to say no. I wrote in my journal the reasons why I was worth way too much to just hand over my YES, and none of them dealt with my awesome work ethic or what I had done for the company previously. None of my reasons made it appear as if there was a deficit within my director's spirit. Nor did I come up with a facade to make it appear as if I was a magical unicorn that could handle any work load they threw at me to "prove my worth." I spoke of myself alone. I spoke of my value and worth. I spoke to how you can really tell the integrity of a being, when that someone is placed in a position of power. I spoke about integrity and not legality. I ushered in words of relationship-building and telling the story of your company from the inside-out.

My director mentioned "big names" of companies that she had worked for before as if that would sway my stance. Even then, I stood firm in my choice, for no name became bigger than the one I gave to myself. Everyone around me got the cue for how to show up in my life from me, and who was I to show them how to mistreat, how to get over, how to devalue, how to make less of my most precious and valuable asset? Me. I laid out instructions, not of *how* they would treat me, but *who* they were treating.

Fear coursed through me, and I moved anyway. I did not lose my job that day, but I stood up for what I believed in and was ready to take the loss if that was in God's plan. We had an in-depth conversation on how my company could support me, instead of the other way around. I had three girls who stayed home waiting and depending on me, with 80 dollars a month in child support, yet I moved anyway. I would have never gone into the office and changed careers on my own accord, but sometimes the observer pushes us out of the nest. I prayed that I would be able to fly before I hit the ground. I flapped my wings and I moved, terrified of each gust of wind or chance of precipitation along the way, and still I moved.

I realized that in order for a problem to exist, there already had to be a solution. That is just one truth of the world we operate in. Not only was it one solution, there were a vast multitude of what choices life could give me, and for the first time, with fear, came excitement, ready for change.

In order to be promoted, you have to move from the space you've been in.

I was so excited to go sign up for a new apartment. I went and visited the main clubhouse which was grand indeed. There were thick, fake Persian rugs and fancy decor. On the inside of the apartment they did not have the tall ceilings I was used to, but there was some crown molding and hardwood floors. The kitchen was beautiful with granite countertops, stainless steel appliances, and a nice island. Everything excited me to move here, and I already had myself and the kids' rooms picked out and decorated in my head. I Google-searched color schemes, and stocked up on wooden shelves at the store. I claimed the apartment and proceeded.

I filled out the application over the weekend, and made my way back to the apartment complex's office, pulled into the drive, got out of the car with my license and blank check in my hand, and headed in the building. But something funny happened. Actually, not so funny, because it stood in the way of what I thought I wanted so badly. Something happened inside me, that when the doorbell rang, as my tennis shoes crossed into the entranceway, I seemingly went into a trance. I walked over the threshold happy and excited for the vision I had for myself and the new journey ahead, but my first instinct told me, "No."

Why was I telling myself no? I couldn't figure the reason. However, I remembered all the times I had not followed my first instinct in the past, and how much I regretted it later on. One thing was for certain, I wouldn't put myself in a situation that might one day lead to an, "I told you so." I was told no, and at first glance, when I looked into the face of the glaring statue before me, I saw a face of evil. When I looked back at the face, the longer I stared at it, the more common, the less frightening and all the more normal it became. This made me relate this lesson of faith onto my own complacency, so I gave myself other possibilities and other perceptions.

How was I supposed to earn my first million by my set timeline, if I locked myself into another year lease? I got the feeling that maybe my dreams had outgrown my current circumstances, and that I would be limiting the flexibility of my choices if I continued to live as I lived before. Maybe, walking by faith meant not binding myself to man's contract, but tying myself to my higher purpose and being. I had a spiritual contract to birth my vision. I became impregnated with purpose that maybe this space, this city, this time couldn't contain. Maybe, all the places I was destined to go within the next year would take me away from those hardwood floors, those granite countertops, and that kitchen island, or maybe, just maybe, I was promoted to become an owner on my own, instead of just a renter of circumstances. I heard a yes, but I felt a no.

I oftentimes think this feeling is the reason why we are to listen to our first mind. This can also be called our gut instinct, depending on whether the response is visceral or logical. Our first mind, is likely God's mind, the connection, and is what we must stop and listen for. But everything you hear is not always from the omnipotent Source. I remember hearing in the news about a boy that went into an African-American Church to murder the members. I recall him saying something like, "I almost didn't go through with it, because they were so nice." What if, he had only listened? What if he had paid more attention to the feeling in his body than the thoughts in his head? We must not be rigid in our judgment or stagnant in our field. We must set out with intention, but at the same time be open to possibility. Life is flexible and so are we. We are meant to be pulled and stretched and contorted in ways we haven't even begun to imagine. If only, we would listen.

DO IT AFRAID

What is it that you are afraid of? I would argue that when most of us say we fear a lack of money, we are also fearful of financial abundance. While we are afraid of being hurt, we are more fearful of finding the love of our lives. We fear working every day to invest our lives within the dreams of others, but are scared to death to walk in and put in our two-week's notice to invest in ourselves. We are afraid of success just as much as we are afraid of failure, and so we look for common ground to lay our head and rest our feet upon. We become tired of the walk and want for nothing more than a drink of water. What we really want is to live in our best lives now, as close to our own version of success as possible. But we give up before the real work even begins, because it seems too daunting. Oh yes, we look around at what's common, what's ritualistic, what's "normal." A place in between the worst-of-the-worst and the best-of-the-best, in which the pleasant dwell with the unpleasant. The place in which you are comforted by others who have given up in the very same way. We are comfortable in complacency, and we sit there for so long we forget to get back up and go back to who we once dreamed we would be. We give the advice that we wish we had the courage to take. Just imagine how we could experience our world if we took our own advice, instead of trying to convert other people into believers of our vision.

When I look back at my life and my relationships and the dreams that weren't watered, I get discouraged to see those same seeds growing and thriving in other people's gardens. I am most discouraged at myself, for not taking advantage of the seeds that were laid before me. Once upon a time, there were dreams bursting from every seam of me. There was a carefree being, but then, as some people say, "Life happened." The oxymoron is, life did anything but "happen." Life stood still for as long as I could remember, not a stillness like prison, that would drive you immediately insane, but a subtle stillness like dementia. It creeps up on you 15 or 20, or maybe even 40 years later, and then you wonder when all the time flew by. An unintentional life is a life that passes you by. But at that time, I held steadfastly to what I was taught as a child. I was taught to go to school, work hard, and to find a backup plan to help me survive instead of thrive. No one ever told me, the backup plan would make me sad, make me nauseated, and make me feel like one day my life wasn't worth living.

Even as adults, there are not many masters to teach us. There are not many places shown to us as possibilities. Therefore, we settle into who we think we are. We base this idea on the principles of what the people who profoundly impacted us told us we needed to be. Well, I really don't want to break this to you, but just because your mother taught you one thing, doesn't mean it's right. Or it may be one right thing amongst a plethora of other equally right possibilities. Don't walk around in your young adult years with all of your eggs in one basket. Young adulthood is when the work of learning begins.

My environment was no longer contained, my community was no longer gated, but I was still a person unwilling to unlearn some lessons. You don't know what you don't know, however you cannot pour into a cup that's already full. If you show up in life thinking you know all the answers, that who you are is always what you were meant to be, you will never be able to evolve. And the craziest thing about fear is that it teaches you to sit stagnant in your being and wait. It teaches you to take the easy road instead of the one less traveled. But no one ever tells you that the easy road, may not lead you to your destiny. We cut off our emotion and knowingness to become a part of the hustle and bustle. And then we wake up one day, depressed, suicidal, and negotiating with ourselves on how much longer we will allow our dreams to die a slow, painful death. In your life, you will not be ready at the same time as everyone else to grow, and at other times you will think that you have it all figured out. But it was in the midst of thinking I had it all figured out, when I finally figured out, I knew nothing at all. For when I stayed in that place of knowing, I blocked my growth and my ability to learn. Fear can be great at shielding us from the unknown, not to rocket you to success, but to keep you in a box, living only to survive.

It is difficult in modern society to follow or adhere to advice blindly. We are result-driven individuals who want to see who made it first. We demand that other people eat, breathe, and sleep the life that they speak, when we do not hold ourselves to those same standards. Not only that, we want physical evidence of how someone else benefited from using their fear as a catapult to greatness before we are willing to buy into it. The only problem with this need for evidence is that it leaves no room for faith, which every great person has had to exercise to get to their place of significance. A life filled with joy and bliss, is not something that can always be seen with the human eye or held in the palm of your hand, or made known by means of material wealth. I know it may be hard to fathom, but not everyone even wants material wealth. Real power does not need to be loud. It is quiet, soft, subtle, and only comes out if needed. Power is bountiful in sharing with itself, it is not boastful or proud. But to get to your power you must overcome your fear.

I thought I would feel giddy with excitement and happiness after leaving the dealership when purchasing my first vehicle; my credit score was higher, there was no cosigner required, the car had only 70 miles on the odometer. When I visualized myself receiving a new car, I had tears of joy in my eyes, and also a reverence of disbelief. This appreciation is the feeling I get when I receive material wealth. I did overall feel a sense of accomplishment, because my outside world began to mimic my inside world, but at the same time the success made me nervous. To my core, success did not make me want to go out and continue working or reaching forward, it made me afraid.

I've had other people tell me they've felt this way too. Clients who were going to receive organ transplants spoke of that overwhelming feeling of dread. Everyone around them was hooting and hollering, grateful for their chance of recovery, but here they were thinking of the surgery, thinking of all the medications they'd have to take for the rest of their lives so their bodies wouldn't reject the organ. They were afraid of a good thing. Quite often I think it is not just the bad "what-ifs" that scare us into complacency, but the good "what-ifs" as well. And so, we sit stuck, not wanting the good or the bad, just sitting in still water so that the boat doesn't rock, tilt, or drift.

I was nervous about success, because reaching my goals meant people would "see me," not just what was on the surface, but what I would have to become committed to show up as. I put myself in the position to be so clear on who I was, so that when people looked at me, all they could see was a mirror reflection of themselves. They would sit at my desk and thumb through my files and take from me whatever they needed. The vulnerability it took to overcome my fear was like a spiritual audit. And the panic that came over me would have caused paralysis if I had let it. If I was ready to lay down my life at the feet of my 9-5 job, and never shoot for the stars, I could have let the discomfort consume me. My body could have become cold from just existing and trying to generate heat to keep itself warm and safe inside of the box where my friends and my family placed me. But what better way to keep me warm than to light my own fire of courage and destroy the evidence of my comfort. Then I could be sure I would not freeze to death from winter. I would be warm, staring into the face of the desire, its alluring flames capturing my gaze, to never let me go. So, I relinquished control of my fear and let my perseverance become the fire. My prior life of mediocrity became the evidence and went up in flames while my courage and I watched the smoke reach unimaginable heights.

See, it was easy to tell everyone else how to believe, how to overcome, how to love themselves, but at the same time I couldn't help but hold the microscope up to my own life to see how I compared. Imagine, after death, on our journey back to the spiritual realm, standing in line and waiting while our good works are weighed against all of our shortcomings. There would surely be some teeth chattering, some nail-biting, some hair twisting, and some elbows knocking. Fingers and toes would be crossed as we awaited our final answer. Was I enough? Did I touch and save more people than I let down and disowned?

The thing is, we are not nervous because we are being judged, we are nervous because we already know the answer. I mean, who knows us better than ourselves? You already know the answers to the questions in your heart. A question cannot even exist without the possibility of answers, and so don't expect the universe to take a break, sit down, and recollect all the things you've done, because I can imagine that you've been keeping tabs on yourself. I don't need a "job well done" plaque to hang on my spiritual wall in my heart space. I created the life, I created the events, I created the time and space in which events occur. Therefore, the question is, why was I nervous? I was nervous because of what someone else told me I could or couldn't be. I was nervous because the risk of my dream was explained to me before I even thought of the idea. I was nervous because everybody else looked happy, living the same life that the majority of people live. I had to ask myself some questions about what I wanted to be known for at the end of my life and I invite you now to ask yourself those same questions.

If this was your last day, and you could not have tomorrow, ask yourself:

Was I an advocate for my true self in my life?

Did I show up for myself authentically when nobody else could?

Did I show up still operating out of fear from what someone told me I could or could not be?

Was I all that I wanted to be every day?

Did I represent what I wanted my life to stand for?

If you are uncertain of any one of these questions, whether your spirit gives you a hard yes or a soft no, then you are ready to leave the abandonment of yourself and your dreams in the past. Don't be afraid to step into your destiny. Instead use your fear to ignite your fire and burn the evidence of all the years you didn't put yourself first.

Today is the first day to start giving the love you have given to everyone else, to yourself.

Use the fear as your catalyst. The experience God has for you and the vision you have set for yourself, may look very different. You have to be prepared to accept blessings without measure. For as long as we are still operating from a place in which we feel we are not enough or that we don't measure up by our own standards, we can only attract people who feel the same things about themselves and us. We can use this fear of failure to propel us into greatness. The fear then becomes intentional, and you can make it yield to your beck and call.

When you become fearless, you stop bonding to other people's brokenness and operating in their field of solidarity.

It's funny, how we can meet someone, and feel that no one else in the world can understand us like they do. It appears that no one could be more empathetic than someone that has been through the same experience as you. If my mother passed away, and your father is dying, we bond over an experience, instead of bonding over love. Or if we both come from single-parent households, we might bond from a place of deficit. This bond, however, does not mean we interpreted the situation the same, that we learned the same things, or that we apply the lessons to our lives in the same way. Just because you weren't taught how to love appropriately as a child, and now you've had a breakthrough and finally get it, does not mean the other person who went through a similar situation is in the same place. In turn, a common bond can result in attracting someone who carries traits opposite of the ones you thought you were looking for. Look to others who are striving to manage their imperfections, otherwise, they will push you, and your transformation backwards. Someone who falls in love with himself all over again is like a shiny, new toy with a fresh coat of paint, waiting to be pushed off the shelf, to someone who doesn't even know what love is. Broken people want to break other people. There is familiarity for them amongst the broken pieces.

Once you give yourself a pass for your past, you change the meaning of your circumstances. When you stop running from the hurt and turn around to look it in the face, you acknowledge all the fear behind you that made you not play full out. There is strength in this acknowledgement, in knowing you didn't always show up for yourself, but today is the first day you will love on yourself like you've loved on everybody else. This is the only way through the hurt, past the blame, and beyond what you may consider a derailment in your life. You will become free to paint a new life on a blank canvas. You can empathize and understand where others are in their journey, but be aware enough to not bond to their struggle. It is then possible to bond to the heart of the person, and if invited, be glad in helping shape them into the whole person they never knew themselves to be.

Now Repeat After Me

I recognize all my stories, are just that, stories. Our lives are an accumulation of stories. I also acknowledge that I am within a level of consciousness that has endless possibilities for whatever I want present in my life. The fear of my past was just an alternate ending. But today I get to choose how my life plays out, because I am the author, the guide, and the master builder, every day in my life.

Fear and Love

So, answer me this, in love-ships, when there are so many good men and women in the world, why waste your time on the one who doesn't return your call? To build a strong house with reinforced walls, a temple for true love to be birthed in, become changed in, and grow up in, you have to take into consideration the structure of the building. I like to visualize the structure of each relationship as if it is built with match sticks. Through this visualization, you can see how each relationship's framework is extremely flammable. When one area starts smoking from friction, it is easy to see how the entire relationship could go up in flames. When thinking of the maintenance of your relationships, consider, if this was the home where the person I loved the most resided, would I bail at the first sign of smoke? Some of us would run into a burning, collapsing building to save the ones we love; however, this puts your life at risk. If your house is on fire, I don't advise leaving the scene, but you may need to create space until the smoke clears, then come back later to see if the damage is reparable. For example, if you are going through a separation in a marriage, as a result of your partner lying about infidelity. You must determine if the house your relationship is built with is smoking or on fire. And the only way to evaluate the extent of the damage is from a distance. If it is on fire, you then have to decide if you are willing to continue running back into the flames at the risk of losing your life.

To build a palace of fortitude with match sticks requires elegance and intention. Each matchstick represents a moment in time when we build our trust with one another. In each experience, we can act out of integrity, compassion, honesty, and love. If with each matchstick you showed how to love more than what to expect of love, maybe some of the walls within your infrastructure wouldn't be so debilitated. If you come into love expecting what you can get instead of what you can give, your matchsticks will be defective and cause a fire during the slightest wind. But if you care more about what someone else needs and how staying connected allows both of your spirits to grow, then you will see the return value in your giving. Each person, in any type of love-ship, comes to the table with their own set of matches, with interaction and consciousness as the glue to hold them all together. When we are not conscious and intentional in what we are building, we start stacking defective pieces.

If you are in a relationship with a healthy, whole individual, most of their matchsticks will be fully functional. They will light quickly near flammable substances. They will be red at the head and wooden at the base. They light quickly when called to action that pulls them deeper into their purpose on the planet. The red on the match head is the God Spark they carry in their spirit that they never allow to dim in the presence of others. And the wooden base represents consistency in their love, consistency in their being, and the ability to put good into the world.

You may have some defective sticks where the base is wooden but splintered, or they are shorter than the rest of the sticks, with evidence that they have already been burned. These defects, although capable of producing an experience that will still bring you to a place of your higher self, may make the process of getting to that place more painful. When you build relationships with defective matchsticks, it is very time consuming, so people lose their patience and they keep getting burned over and over again. We should never bring along with us sticks that have already been burned when building a new house. The finished house might look good on paper, in pictures, and on social media, but it will not assist you in sustaining a heavy rain. Unrestored matchsticks leave cracks, crevices, and leaks that weaken your foundation, and if left unchecked or repaired, may one day leave you homeless. Then every stick is lost, the good along with the defective, and people are left looking into the mirror wondering where the time went and where all the scars came from.

Some people may be content with the defects. Some people love the challenge of fixing up and restoring old houses. But anyone will tell you, it's a lot of work. Maybe more work than you'd like to admit you'd bargained for. Are you willing to enter into an intimate relationship with a partner with low self-esteem? Or how about someone who was sexually assaulted or has issues with their parents? Some people love their old house so much, because it's one they've built from the ground up. Most people want a work they can look back on and be proud of. Sometimes, if they are not fully committed to taking pride in their work, they place their value of the structure in the time they spent creating it; quantity over quality. So, in this way, the work is defective but they will not put the house up for sale. They have lived there for so long, they cannot imagine where else would they go. Even if they can imagine it, the house they are in scares them, but a new house frightens them too.

So, they sit still, a prisoner to their own fear. Another thing about fear is that it produces a consistent pain. Because they know what to expect, people stay in the discomfort of dysfunction. What type of house have you built with people you are in relationship with? Is it one out of dysfunction or one out of destiny?

Become clear on what you want in your life; also, be clear of who you are outside of human relationships, but in relationship with the Creator. Some of us need to trade in some of our matchsticks. A relationship with a Source greater than yourself is an excellent way to restore your box. If you are not clear on what you want present in your life, all sorts of dysfunction will show up in your relationships and replace peace with its normality. When an employer hires an employee, there is normally a time at which the employer expects the employee to be present at work. If there is no schedule, people do not know when to show up. When the schedule is handed out, maybe the employee is tardy. The first couple of tardies may initiate a warning, but eventually, if you are not intentional enough to show up to work on time, you will get pulled into the office and receive corrective action. If the unwanted behavior continues, eventually the employer will end your relationship. Maybe your values are placed in money and not in love. So, you're on time for work, but not on time for date night. However, if you are to be a giver and a receiver of real love you have to give people the blueprint of what you expect. More importantly you must know in the blueprint what you are willing to accept. And just like the employer, if your boundaries are crossed there must be a course of action to correct the disorder that person brings into your life. You are the first person to show people in your life how to treat you.

Show me your work, and I'll show you your passion.

Now, I've heard some people say to me that they don't want to treat their relationship like work. They believe that an intimate relationship should be easy, and that setting intention makes it less romantic. I am a huge fan of romance, but I am also a huge fan of allowing each person to feel safe in a relationship and intentionally giving what the other person needs. First, this must be communicated, and again it comes down to your perception about what you place value in. When we don't see the value or a rate of return for our deposits, then we do not feel safe. A relationship between you and your boss, or you and a company, requires communication with your manager to receive reimbursement for services provided. Should one work, not be paid, and continue to show up? It doesn't matter how much you love your job, you will still require monetary compensation to feed your family. So, why is it that since the reimbursement we receive in our interpersonal relationships is not monetary, it becomes less valuable?

Lying in bed all day may not pay the bills, but we were not put here to pay bills in the first place. So, go out and work for what you're worth, but never forget where you came from and who is most important.

If our relationships with people generated money or precious jewels, real estate or networking, would we finally see them as beneficial? Why do our love-ships get the short end of the stick when placed in comparison with our business relationships? Because we think making money is hard and love should be easy. But what if I told you, the intention to love is most essential. What if I told you that making money is easy, but maintaining healthy, mutually beneficial relationships is not. Even though healthy relationships reap the biggest rewards of life, that is where most inner change and self-work resides.

If you have a block in this area of your life, you must become intentional about clearing the block. How you know you have a block is, if in this particular area, you keep attracting different partners with the same characteristics. You want to be single but have told yourself, "Maybe being single is just not meant for me." You want to have children but have not met the one to start a family with. If you are not single "on purpose," you may have a block. If you seem to be getting the same outcome in any given situation, there is a block in your subconscious mind. This block is your own little personal "hell on earth." At times, you think you've cleared a belief, but may not have cleared all the residual that comes along with it. For example, my original core belief from the time I was about three years old was that I was abandoned. I forgave my mother, didn't really think anything about it, and went on with my life, or so I thought. There was a period in my life that I was only attracted to men who wouldn't do what they said they would. They said they were going to call later, then never called. They gave me scenarios of how our relationships were to progress, for the sake of telling me what I wanted to hear, but I could tell their hearts weren't in it. I was the center of attention of during our courting period, but then they would suddenly become too busy to stop by when they only lived five minutes away; great people who lacked integrity. What made it more strange, was that there was a common theme among each of these men when I sat down and examined all the parts of my creation. There was a string of events within me, and the biggest one that stood out was that I picked all of the men. None of them chose me, I chose them. But apparently, I chose wrong.

From the time I had my first boyfriend, I never went more than a couple of months as single. I searched for someone to blame, yet there was no one but me. I was sending out the "available" signal, and the worst part about it was they didn't even have to approach me. I basically grabbed them by the hand, with my spirit screaming, "Come on, Baby. Let me show you how to mistreat me." They mistreated and in turn abandoned me because on the inside I mistreated and abandoned myself. In a desperate need to obtain a family, since I had never felt like I belonged to one, I attempted to create one with people who couldn't care less. This was the residual of my abandonment. I had forgiven my mother for dropping me off and never picking me back up, but who knew that my desire for my own family would sabotage the very thing I wanted the most?

Any act from a desperate place will only produce greater desperation. And I didn't attract abandonment because I wanted to be left alone again. I tracked loss by the amount of energy I put into not wanting to be left again. I tried to safeguard my relationships to make sure nothing bad would happen. I wanted the family I never believed I had, and I was desperate to get it and fight to maintain it. But all I was left fighting for was myself, for no other person believed in the dream I had for the family, but me.

Relationships for me were not always this way. Believe you me, I've had a couple men, totally in love with me, that I mistreated along the way. But apart from every other area in my life, I still was not in a place where I fully trusted myself to receive everything I wanted. When I visualized what I wanted, I second-guessed whether I was ready for love, or whether I deserved to be in a relationship with the type of man I attracted. I knew somewhere along the way, I picked up a parasite, a block, a misfortune, however you'd like to name it, that prevented me from gaining everything I felt I wanted and deserved.

Whenever I ask Divine guidance a question, I receive the answer. We must hone in on which are the correct questions to ask.

The answer was, that somewhere along the way, there was something or someone I had not forgiven for their perceived mistreatment of me. And so, my love life was on a loop. I began to examine and explore a vast multitude of possibilities. I asked Divine guidance what those possibilities might be, and through my daily spiritual practice, I received answers that shocked me. I had lack of residual forgiveness that I wasn't even aware of. I invite you now, to ask the right questions and then to sit in silence long enough to receive the answer. Write out the crazy answers too; we don't want to block our breakthroughs, by refusing to give things possibility.

The problem in our society is that we are too focused on being a filter and not a funnel Let the universe pour into you, not through you.

Some unexpected answers that came up for me were, "Since I never even had the opportunity of meeting my biological father, had I forgiven him for not being present?" I never thought to forgive the absence of someone I never met. Some would say, you can't miss what was never present, but you can miss it and not even know it.

Another residual was that I was evicted from my home. For a short period of time I was homeless, but I told myself I was free and that it didn't bother me. But it did bother me, because when the first mate came along with a secure environment, I had a problem letting go. I did not love him more than I loved finally having a safe, quiet place to rest my head at night.

I remember one Valentine's Day when my first daughter was still little. I headed out to work, and I gave her father a Valentine's Day card. He said thank you, but did not get me anything in return. I was emotional and saddened and felt he didn't care for me. I expressed this to him, saying, "You didn't get me anything?" He got upset with me, and we started arguing. He told me how ungrateful I was because he provided a home for us. He told me to pack my things and to get out of his house. Later when I examined the situation I realized, I hadn't forgiven all the secrets in our relationship, I hadn't forgiven the leaving, and most of all I never forgave him for telling me to leave "his" house with our toddler baby girl. I had a difficult time letting go of the family I worked so hard to build, but I built it on my own. I believed when people called you their soul mate and stared into your eyes, saying they would never leave, that life would give me just what they said. I believed we had a soul contract. I put so much merit in the word of a man, that I forgot the word that lived in me. From this place, I realized that those things I didn't want in our relationship continued, and my relationships did not improve. I had a block from my fear of being without a family and homeless, so I attracted this fight over and over again. And one of the most effective ways to prohibit the block from showing up again was through forgiveness.

And so, I say to you, Forgive Everyone for Everything.

YOUR GOD SPARK

It is my belief that each of us carries a flame, burning within us like the Olympic torch. I in no way infer my own beliefs onto others. So, no matter your belief system, what you name the source from which you came, the universe, the source, a deity, or God, does not matter. But for conversational purposes and from my own point of view, I call my source God. What all is created from, operating within, and will ever be, is an ever-present energy force. Since we are all a part of this energy field, made completely of the same molecules, having the same electrical conduction in our nervous system firing off sparks between our synaptic clefts, it is plausible that we are all source manifested in the flesh. And within that flesh you have what modern medicine considers organs and tissues, arteries, veins, and capillaries, cell membranes and mitochondria, derived from atoms and ions. With a large enough microscope, we can see that the individual makeup of our housing systems, our bodies, are all built from the same "stuff." Everything, including you and me, is made up of energy.

What most people have a difficult time coming to grasp with is what appears to be solid or different from us. We are so accustomed to being individual and special, we want to stand apart from other beings and separate ourselves from the world. But when God created it all, the pen was made no different from the car, the hand no different from the clouds, and the trees no different from the lungs. The lungs exchange gas just like the trees, and such is the rhythm of life. The molecules surrounding us determine how they want to be present in our lives by the energy we exert in thought and in creation. What we pay attention to and how we respond to the stimuli placed in front of us determines its value in our lives.

We have the power to give our tears meaning and purpose. So, you must ask yourself the question, how much is your spirit of creation worth to you? Are you willing to hand it over for the presence of another person? This power is and will forever be your most valuable asset. Spirit is something that cannot be seen with current visual rods and cones or heard with current auditory canals and drums. We give ourselves meaning and purpose and determine the extent of our own happiness, the impact of our undercurrent, the presence radiating from our being. It is never, and I do mean never, necessary to dim you fire, your spirit, your "God Spark" within the presence of others.

We have been taught from some of our parents, from some of our religions, from some of our world leaders and mentors, gurus and prophets, that to give and to put other's needs before our own, to be sacrificial, is to be holy. In order to be whole and holy, we must deny ourselves certain worldly pleasures, and it just so happens that one of those pleasures is the caring and nurturing of ourselves. I am here to tell you, that there is room at the table for everyone to have a seat, to come sit amongst the greatness, to share in the abundance and learn the secrets of how to remember who we really are. There is no need to push each other down to get to the feast; there is no need to share your food to be liked by everyone else. You have your own special seat, because there is a treat that we only get to feed from when you are present. You are meant to be there and if anyone asks you to give up your seat because they like your view better than they like their own, be as still as the queen or king you are.

There is a fire burning within you, a God Spark. It is at the end of every synaptic cleft, the electricity that fires with each beat of your heart, and at the tips of your fingers when you come in contact with certain places, people, and things. Sometimes you may laugh it off and say, "You shocked me" sometimes we use the artificial shock we've created to externally stop your heart in hopes it will start up again on its own. Sometimes we give up on our spark and it slows what we can do in our bodies by decreasing our ability to fight off infections, or our ability to make new tissue, or new white blood cells until it decimates entirely. However, there is a spark carried within you at all times. Where we get into trouble, is in our attempt to extinguish the flame. Sometimes our flame burns so brightly, and other times it becomes intolerable to your temperament and temperature. We must continue to stand out so that it feels safe to take up room.

I like to visualize my God Spark in the center of my chest. When I look to my brothers and sisters I can see their sparks burning ferociously. When we first come into contact with a romantic interest, for instance, our fires burn like wild amidst dry forest brush. This flame could only be described as a spark, considering the source it was created from, like a sparkler next to the sun. This is the fire that makes up who we are, a spiritual flame. This space is where being on fire for your purpose is ignited and stays lit.

The Olympic flame continually burns, but when it rains, the fire may sputter as if running out of fuel. If there isn't enough fuel, that fire may eventually die out. There are forces that will come into your life like rain in springtime. Sometimes it may seem like it's raining every day. This rain may present itself as depression, abandonment, low self-esteem, fear of failure, or fear of loss. But we cannot stop or complain about the rain. And just like in springtime, we need every little drop of rain, to excavate our soil, to saturate our heirloom seeds, to infuse kind words and the love we deserve. We need the ground, soaking wet. It won't rain all the time, and therefore once the sun comes out, we see the baby green coming from the grooves of the earth; this is the earth within us. The earth is our physical body, the sun is the greater flame from which our spark derives, and the baby green; the truth manifested through experience.

What I have found to be a truth within my own life, is when our spark diminishes, it can either occur from one of two levels of consciousness, willingly or unwillingly. Both produce devastating but very vital effects to your spiritual well-being. When your spark diminishes you are not yourself. And when this happens in the presence of other people, we create some of the most toxic and unfulfilling relationships of all time.

For example, Chris met Johanna and loved everything about her. Her self-confidence and energy were through the roof, and this energy was what attracted Chris to her initially. They spoke to each other every day, but Johanna had feelings of abandonment from an overly critical mother during childhood, and instead of taking responsibility for her own happiness or fulfilling the hole that was already present within her, Chris became the anchor for her joy. When she heard from him her eyes sparkled and it sent a sense of calm down her spine from the release of her anticipation.

This was an unhealthy and subconscious/unwilling, self-diminishing of Johanna's spark. She was giving away her own self-love and didn't even know it. So, when Chris didn't call and she felt upset, she vested her emotional well-being into the hands of another. No one external of you should have enough power over you to determine how your day is going to go. The only person responsible for you and your happiness is you.

Another example, with Chris and Johanna, is that after they met Chris was everything Johanna had looked for. He always made her feel like a priority. Their dates were planned a week ahead, and they spent as much time together as possible. Every time they were together, it was almost like they were a part of each other. Then one day, they had an argument over Chris wanting to have an open relationship. Johanna's feelings were hurt, but in an attempt to regain, not the quality, not the integrity, but the presence of her ideation of what her real-life Prince Charming would be, Johanna agreed. This agreement became a conscious/willing decision to hand over her energy, her power, and diminish her spark, because she was willing to pretend the new relationship boundary was something she was okay with.

The problem in itself not only lies in the giving away of a prize that could never be earned. Some things of this world are more precious than wealth, worth more than a witness, worth more than fame. You are your own witness. And the unease within both parties involved originates from a loss of identity.

Once your spark starts to cower, or make itself smaller to fit into a space that other people created for it to exist, you start to become less and less of your true self. At times it can get to the point where you are no longer recognizable; not to others, and even more sadly not to yourself. You may commonly hear people who look in the mirror at the end of a long-term relationship that they fought to keep together, saying to themselves, they don't even know who they are anymore. They've lost so much of themselves in the relationship, trying to appease the other person, that they have neglected themselves. In reality, it is never the other person we are trying to please. We are trying to fill a gap, build a bridge across the river of abandonment, hoping that person's life force will pour into us and fill us up. But people tend to not take kindly to the draining of their life-force. People don't like to be used as the temporary numbing agent for your pain. They will lash out when their energy is depleted out of basic self-preservation and do almost anything to get you to leave their presence. While your spark is shape-shifting or changing colors, your nature falters and becomes unrecognizable. Pretty soon you find yourself waking up beside and within a stranger.

If I was in the grocery store shopping, and someone came up from behind me and attempted to hold my purse for me, I'd be really uncomfortable. Heck, I might even start yelling, kicking, slapping, screaming for help, and basically doing anything to draw attention to myself, so maybe someone could come help me hold on to my belongings. This reaction is the same response you will get in relationships, when your spark is dimmed and you become unrecognizable. Once you become so out of character, that your God Spark is only a dimly lit dollar store candle; once you have demoted yourself in another's presence, or even worse, your flame lies on the ground dormant, you wait for two rocks to strike and ignite some vibration within you. You are dead inside, and then, its battle time. Your flame is now the equivalent to the capacity of the pop-its we give to our kids on the 4th of July. Little stones, surrounded by powder and tissue paper. You can squeeze it between your fingers, because the combustible force is so small and insignificant, it doesn't even begin to frighten you. Once your spark is nearly extinguished, the attack begins from the people you are closest in relationship to.

When you can no longer recognize the person standing before you on a spiritual level, you become angry because a complete stranger is kicking their feet up on your coffee table. The loss of your identity becomes a fight, sometimes, until the death of mutualism, the loss of connection, the destruction of shared values and dreams. It's a boxing fight, knuckles dragging across the pavement, bloody and mangled, as the both of you attempt to crawl your way back into the sunlight to reignite your flame. One person is unable to reignite their flame, because they gave it all away; the other person, because they've used the both of you up, trying to fill an endless void within themselves. And you thought that maybe letting them borrow a little, or that pouring some of your spark into them would make both of you full?

Each being is born with the God Spark; it is the energy that causes cell division and multiplication. I urge you to be in the company of others who allow you to be your greatest self at all times. Other people, whose fires burn ferociously beside yours, so that they playfully compete in grandiosity and cause both of you to grow. Never turn your back on the ones who run towards you with their fists ready and face painted, screaming their battle cry at the first sign of smoke. These people are thieves, trying to steal your spark. You must become a warrior when it comes to protecting your light.

When questioning if a person is to remain in your life, look not to your own understanding. Your spark is connected to the greater source and the answer you seek has been inside you all along. Ask yourself, and give your body permission to accept the answer and act on it as it comes. Never make decisions quickly or with haste, and when you don't know what to do, do nothing.

When you can no longer hear the voice of the Source, ask yourself, is it because I have not been still enough or quiet enough for long enough? It is within the quiet of the wind and sparkles amidst a navy-blue sky, that we hear you most, Lord. While everyone else is sleeping, let us stay awake waiting, to hear what is the next right thing that the creator wants us to do.

With the Source as your guide, acknowledge that you created the life you wanted to exist, before life even knew it existed. You are a supernatural being, unrepeatable, a body where things happen through you, not to you. You became so consumed in the doing, so committed to the story, so enchanted by the offense that you held onto things that no longer serve your higher purpose. But here is where we leave that story, we hand it back to the person that gave it to us. Here is where we say, no more.

To Break Bravely means to hurt and to release. We couldn't reach our greatest peak until we hit rock bottom. We could not grow to love who we are today without each thought, each tragedy, and each person of our yesterday. We could not be closer to resembling God if we didn't go through our days experiencing all the beautiful, small, but carefully crafted pieces that make up the great I, AM. We are at a granular level of a grand plan, reaching to express the greatest light that we forgot we always possessed. With each day we are damaged but determined, enraged but enlightened, in the worst of times and the best of times. We are Breaking Bravely.

About The Author

Stacie Winkfield is a Licensed Registered Nurse and a Business Branding and Personal Development Coach that teaches her clients unique techniques on how to Break Bravely into their Best Life. She helps her clients go from having an imposter syndrome to showing up as confident world leaders and becoming the brand that everyone loves to follow. As a result of working with her, Stacie's clients are able to move past self-limiting beliefs, create a committed tribe of supporters, and show up in the world as they explore their beauty in ways they could have never imagined.

This is the first of Stacie's Best-Selling Book Series, Breaking Bravely. Her second Relationship-Edition is due to be released in mid-2018. She is also a contributing author to an Anthology which will be published in February 2018. This work includes authors from around the world sharing their stories about entrepreneurs overcoming adversity. Her greatest joy is seeing lives transformed by the stories of those told around us.

Visit her at www.breakingbravely.com

Stacie lives with her three children in Michigan, along with her American Eskimo dog P-Jelly, and her committed obsession with movie theater popcorn.

There is limited space available for Stacie's "Breaking Bravely Into Your Best Life" Masterclass Coming 2018, which meets on Zoom once weekly for nine weeks. This class dives deeper into each chapter from the book, with weekly group coaching calls, accountability partners, and release from the toxic relationships with others and self-sabotaging behaviors. This is a course focused on falling madly in love with yourself, as if you are meeting yourself for the first time. Sign up for the masterclass at **www.breakingbravely.com/masterclass**

Get Free Training and Coaching online
https://www.breakingbravely.com/staciespeaks

Find Stacie on Social Media:
Join Us At the Breaking Bravely Facebook Page:
https://www.facebook.com/BreakingBravely

Follow her on Instagram @stacie_winkfield
Email her at maximizeyourcapacity@gmail.com

www.ingramcontent.com/pod-product-compliance
Lightning Source LLC
Chambersburg PA
CBHW030841090426
42737CB00009B/1063

9 780692 998144